Focused Financial Literacy

The Starting Point for Financial Success

Blake Reed

from various sources. Please consult a licensed professional before attempting any techniques outlined in this book.

By reading this document, the reader agrees that under no circumstances is the author responsible for any losses, direct or indirect, that are incurred as a result of the use of the information contained within this document, including, but not limited to, errors, omissions, or inaccuracies.

Table of Contents

Introduction: What Is This Book About?

Money. They say it makes the world go round.

When we were younger, we undoubtedly believed that money probably did grow on trees. Why? Well, whenever we wanted something like a new toy, trainers, or a school bag, money was always there. We didn't really know where money came from or why it's important, but we knew it *materialised* our needs and wants. Life was much simpler back then.

In school, you may have begun to understand the basic value of money. What could you do with your weekly pocket money? Spend it immediately, or save it for those cool new trainers everyone is wearing? You learn how to make decisions with your money, and you base it on what is important to you—this is where you begin to become more aware of your values. At this stage in your life, a new toy didn't mean as much as getting new trainers, having money to hang out with your friends, or paying for a film ticket, popcorn, and an extra-large

Coke. That's what matters as a teenager. You had more responsibilities, but it was still simple.

Onto the next stage: University. You're kind of on your own now. You need money for clothes, food, fuel, fees, textbooks, and most definitely, a social life. Monthly allowances from your parents just don't make the cut anymore. So, maybe it's time to look for a job to support your buzzing lifestyle. Aside from knowing where to spend your money, you become aware of why money is an important part of life—it makes things possible. Now, you're learning how to make money and how to spend it responsibly. It's hard at first, because everything is so tempting, but because you're the one earning money, you begin to value it more. As a university student, though, we don't blame you if you got reckless at times. It is a fun and carefree stage of our lives, after all.

When the fun is over, it's time to get serious, like, really serious. You get a real job, and your first real salary, plus, a new flat, maybe a car, and a fresh new professional look. With new needs comes more expenses. It's no longer just about money as a means to buy things, but as a medium to *sustain* your lifestyle. You're bound to have some teething problems in the initial stages. Maybe your income is not growing at quite the same pace as your expenses, and it's a struggle to make ends meet, but you're managing, for now. This is a good time to reevaluate your finances. You read somewhere that the best way to save is to put 10% of your salary away every month. Your savings journey starts. Adulting, right?

As you move on with life, your relationship with money gets more complicated. At this point you're not sure if you love it or you hate it, you just know you need it. Your salary has been steadily increasing, but again, it's not quite enough to keep your lifestyle going. It's been tough to strike a fair balance between life and money. Perhaps you're now at a stage of your life where you're ready to settle down with your special someone. Congratulations on making it this far!

You're entering an exciting new chapter. You and your partner may be looking for a house, plus there's the cost of the wedding. Thank goodness you have some savings. This is your money as a store of value. You also have to adjust your lifestyle for your partner, and now that there's two of you, expenses are bound to rise. Soon children will come into the picture, and you'll have to start thinking about their needs: Clothing, education, and recreation. You're also thinking about retirement. How much money will you need to put aside to retire comfortably? Maybe it's time to get help from a financial advisor, but you heard they also charge money. So, what next? How does one actually obtain an understanding of finances (particularly personal finances)? How can one become 'literate' in the world of finance, and navigate it effectively?

This is where my journey toward financial literacy began. As a single parent, I didn't know how I would provide for my child. I struggled to strike a balance between work, life, and parenting. With so much on my plate and few resources, I had to start thinking about making more money quickly. It was tough to get started, but to my surprise, it got easier with time. I realised that managing your finances is not as complicated as the world makes it seem. I learnt that money is *not* the root of all evil, nor does it bring happiness. I used to think money was the most important thing, but now I understand that it's only as important as I make it. Money became secondary to my time. The moment I changed my thinking around money, the way I used money began to change—with the right tools and knowledge, I took control over my money, my money stopped controlling me.

In *Focused Financial Literacy, The Starting Point for Financial Success,* I will be sharing the knowledge that I gained about the value of money and how you can learn to use it in a positive and healthy way.

I learnt how to use my money more effectively. I paid more attention to where my money was going, where it *should* go, and how to balance the two. It takes patience and practice, but once you find your method, financial literacy is just a few steps away.

Focused Financial Literacy, The Starting Point for Financial Success seeks to help YOU discover your relationship with money to best use it to serve you.

What Is Money and Where Does it Come From?

Money, as *we* know it, is used to buy and sell goods and services. It's a medium of exchange. It's used to make transactions. Currency is not the same as money. Currency is the tangible coin or note you keep in your pocket used to make the physical exchange.

Money does not exist in a vacuum; you can have as many notes or coins as you want, but it only becomes useful when value is placed on it. Usually, it's humans who decide how much a dollar or pound is worth. A number of factors influence it, including international agreements, exchange rates, central banks, and inflation. We will expand more on this in Chapter 1.

Before coins and notes existed, transactions took place through a method called bartering. Bartering is the direct exchange of goods or services—instead of coins, early hunter gatherers used commodities as a medium for exchange. For example, a weapon would be exchanged for a hunted animal, or farmers exchanged a pail of goat's milk for hens. The agreement of exchange was usually a lengthy process because each party had to decide if they were getting their commodities' worth. A standard value system did not exist in the early periods of bartering, so it was the people themselves who decided how much something was worth. Stones, salt, cocoa, rice grains, animal skin, and other commodities were later used as a currency.

Around 770 B.C., the Chinese created replicas of the bigger tools to use as a medium of exchange for practicality and convenience. Eventually, these objects were replaced with round objects—the first known coin, which we still use today. We will expand more on the history of money in Chapter 1.

Money has become more than just a method of trade and exchange—we use money to make money. That's called wealth creation. In *Focused Financial Literacy, The Starting Point for Financial Success,* we will look at the different ways you can make your money work for you, instead of the other way around. It's easier than you think.

We can create wealth, not just by working a 9–5 job, but by exploring the different methods of investing and saving, as we will discuss in this book. You will realise just how easy it is to grow your money if you know where to put it. In Chapter 4 of *Focused Financial Literacy, The Starting Point for Financial Success,* you will be introduced to the methods to help you build your wealth. You have the choice to invest in cash, bonds, companies, commodities, and property—the magic of interest will take your wealth to new heights.

As you kickstart this financial journey, prepare to make changes in the way you save and spend your money. We can all have as much money as we want or need, but what's important is how *you* decide to make use of it.

Your decisions come from your knowledge about how money works and then by understanding your own relationship with it—do you love it or hate it? Does it make a difference in your life? Or how has it changed your life?

On this journey, you will have to ask yourself some really important questions, some that will make you unlearn old habits, break old cycles, and renew your relationship with the money in your pocket.

Your money has power, but you have the power to use it in the right way. With the help of Focused *Financial Literacy, The Starting Point for Financial Success,* by Blake Reed, you will learn how to unleash that power.

Chapter 1:

Even Money Has a

Backstory

Reach into your wallet and pull out a £20 note. What do you see when you look at it? The first would probably be the face of Queen Elizabeth II. Do you know why her picture is on our money?

The Queen is the monarch of Great Britain and the head of state. She is head of the Church of England and a leader in times of crises. Monarchs traditionally appeared on coinage as an authorisation and guarantee of genuine value. It has now become traditional since the Bank of England was given the monopoly of note issue. This is why she is on our money. Does her face make the money more valuable, though? No. Money's value is determined by people and trust.

Money is not to be confused with currency. Money is a non-tangible concept used for exchange. Currency is the tangible object, like your coins and notes, that you use to make a monetary exchange.

So, what is money, where does it come from and what does it do?

Money has three main functions:

1. It serves as a globally accepted medium of exchange. It is used to make transactions.

2. It measures value numerically. When we think of money, we think about it in terms of pounds and pence. These are called denominations of money and they signify money's amount.

3. Money as a store value. Money doesn't just exist in the present. It evolved from the past, and it will evolve in the future. Money can be put away in the form of an investment, and it will grow in value overtime.

Money cannot be altered. Its form can change, from commodities to coins, plastic money, and cryptocurrency. The value of money can change by the day or even by the minute, depending on how it's connected to global markets or a country's monetary system. Money's value only exists because of trust. Trust between people, banks, and traders. Without value, money is nothing more than just a paper or a coin. It will not hold the power to buy anything.

The Origins of Money

Bartering is the first form of trade recorded by archeologists. In simple terms, it's the direct exchange of goods between two parties. Early hunter gatherers only employed the practice of bartering to sustain their livelihoods. The items exchanged depended on the resources available to each party. For example, one group of hunter gatherers could hunt and the other had the resources to make the tools. Both parties needed each other's expertise, so they came up with a method of exchange and trade. Trade and exchange took place on the basis of trust between two parties, and because a standard value system did not apply, the parties themselves would decide if what they were giving was worth what they were receiving.

The articles of exchange evolved overtime, from livestock and weapons to cocoa, textiles, grain, precious metals, and anything that one party *needed,* and the other party *had.* Bartering still exists in different forms today—especially between different countries.

Bartering became more popular, but it became impractical to carry, for example, a huge dead animal on your back. To eliminate that, the method of exchange needed to be altered. It was said that the Chinese in 770 B.C. started making replicas of weapons and other materials that had been cast in bronze to facilitate exchanges. The sharp edges of a weapon were replaced by a disk, which would later become known as the first form of a coin. To make those coins into a more viable and popular form of exchange, a little-known region called Lydia, now Western Turkey, started manufacturing coins in 600 B.C. These coins were traded across borders. Europe was one of the regions to use Lydia's currency.

The coins were made from a mixture of silver and gold and stamped with pictures of animals that acted as denominations to signify the amount, a practice that's being used even now.

Coins were, and still are, a useful form of transaction because of its durability and portability. Coins are not easily damaged or destroyed, and that makes them a valuable form of currency. But too many coins can be burdensome, so paper money was introduced.

In 700 B.C. China started using paper money. This was also in a bid to alleviate the weight of carrying around clunky coins in pockets and bags. Coins were transferred to a trustworthy individual, who would then return a paper note denoting its worth, which could then be used to make future transactions. Two currencies were circulating: Paper and coins. IOUs were also developed when coins or notes could not be immediately exchanged. These are our modern-day credit and debits.

The value system of money can be dated back to the use of precious coins. For example, before 1971, America's banknotes were pegged to a certain amount of gold, which was controlled by the Federal Reserve, but now, the US's paper money is considered fiat money, meaning that it has no actual value—it only fulfills the purpose of making an exchange.

A Lesson on The Value of Money

Europe wasn't introduced to paper money until the late 17th Century. They were still fixated on the use of coins, mainly because of the material that coins were made of: Gold.

Gold is the universal language of the rich, and that still resonates today—but what good is gold if it only shines, right? The history of Spanish 'conquistadors' will explain why.

Conquistadors, which translates to 'conquer,' was a group of around 400 mainly Spanish men who embarked on a journey to colonise and loot the New World back in the 16th Century. The New World is now referred to as the Americas—it comprises North, West, and South America. Christopher Columbus discovered the New World in 1492 and sang its praises for its riches and gold.

During the time lived Spanish King Ferdinand, who, like all kings, wanted to be rich and influential. He heard about the riches that lay in the New World and asked his men to "get gold, humanely, if you can, but at all hazards to get gold" (Davenport, 2012). He wanted as much gold as he could to spread Christianity to non-believers in the Americas. He needed a vast amount of wealth to achieve this and obtaining large amounts of gold was the only answer to this. King Ferdinand sent his men on this great expedition to find gold and bring it back to his kingdom. Seeking gold became a custom, it continued even after King Ferdinand retired from his position.

The conquistadors are not remembered for their bravery, but instead for their ruthlessness. They used their weapons and steel armor in their conquest of the New World. They colonised land and killed people along the way. Conquistadors trekked mainly through what we now know as South America, in regions like Chile, Puerto Rico, Mexico, Cuba, and others. Their main prize, however, was the Incan Empire—one of the largest and richest empires in pre-Columbian America. Inca is now known as Peru.

Inca accumulated a lot of gold through its own conquests and through assimilation with its neighbors, but the people of Inca also knew how to mine gold. Gold was associated with the sun God Inti, whom Incas worshipped and kept the gold for. The Temple of the Sun was described by one Spanish contemporary as "a mine of gold." The rays of the sun were reflected in every direction, which lit up the entire temple. The deity was engraved on a massive plate of gold, covered in a thick layer of emeralds and precious stones (Davenport, 2012).

King Atahualpa, who ruled the Incan Empire, was said to have stored an extensive amount of Inca's wealth. The conquistadors learnt about the Incan Empire and its plentiful wealth. So, in 1526, Francisco Pizarro led an expedition to the Incan Empire to extract gold from the natives.

He captured Emperor Atahualpa amid mass killings in Cajamarca, a city in Peru.

Pizarro asked the emperor to fill up a large room once with gold and twice with silver in exchange for his freedom. The emperor complied with Pizarro's conditions and filled a room with the riches. Pizarro took the riches and killed the emperor anyway. The emperor's ransom amounted to 13,000 pounds of gold and around 26,000 pounds of silver. This still wasn't enough for the conquistadors, who went on to loot Cuzco, the capital city of Inca. The soldiers who worked under Pizarro received a handsome portion of the looting: Each received about 45 pounds of gold and twice that much silver.

Further north in Mexico, conquistadors under the leadership of Hernan Cortés found other great golden treasures, including discs of gold, masks, jewelry, and even gold dust and bars. Sources say they, however, retrieved much less than the army in Inca, but some believed that Cortés hoarded the riches for himself.

More conquistadors decided to visit the Americas upon hearing about the vast amount of gold hidden in the terrains. These conquistadors embarked on separate expeditions in search of more gold. Natives were enslaved along the way. Conquistadors arrived between 1519 and 1540, and it was only until the 1800s that the last conquistadors stopped their search. They lost some of the gold on their way back to Spain, but they still had enough.

Spain's ambition was to become rich, so they decided to melt the gold into coins. Lydia was the first country to mint coins and by the time the Spaniards discovered coins as a form of currency, other countries had already moved to paper money. For the Spanish, the gold was worth more. The crown also intended to use the gold to fund the expenses of maintaining the empire. The more gold they owned, the more coins they minted. This increased the number of coins moving about for trade and exchange of goods. The Spaniards were so concerned with the material of the coins but did not care for the actual value of it. Without value, the coins were near worthless. They couldn't use it for anything in Spain.

When there is a high supply of money moving about in the economy, the money itself loses its value. As a result, inflation soars, and so does the cost of living. At the time, less gold was making its way to Spain, so they could no longer fund its expensive imperial projects. There was increased pressure on the fiscus, and Spain's economy suffered a collapse.

How Value Is Measured

Any material, including but not limited to animals and weapons to grains, cocoa, and textiles, can be used as a currency during trade and exchange. "It is an economic truism that money can be anything that is offered for a thing offered or a thing desired, and Webster's dictionary defines it as anything customarily used as a medium of exchange and measure of value" (Seeger, 1978).

Bartering in the form of exports and imports of raw materials or products still takes place today. For example, spices from India, coffee beans from Vietnam, and rich minerals and metals from South Africa are traded across the globe.

In America, for example, the value of money is determined by the demand for it, and there are three ways to measure the value of the dollar:

- **Exchange rates**: The value of one country's currency against the currency of another nation or economic zone. Exchange rates tell you how much your money is worth in another country. Forex traders on the foreign exchange trading market look at movements of investments to determine the exchange rate of a currency. Oftentimes, an exchange rate fluctuates, and other times, depending on the nation's policies, it is fixed.

- **Treasury notes:** These come in the form of bills, notes, and bonds issued by the US Department of the Treasury. They are a safe and stable form of investment because they are guaranteed by the US Government. The Treasury Department auctions off treasury notes at a fixed interest rate. Bidders are willing to pay more for bills that are in high demand at a fixed rate, as it makes a good long-term investment with better returns.

- **Foreign exchange reserves**: This is the amount of dollars held by foreign governments. The value of the dollar increases when foreign governments hold more dollars because demand for the currency increases. If those governments sell these dollars, it could have an adverse effect on the US economy because it will give rise to inflation.

That's the bigger picture, but how does it affect you?

When money has a low value, there is a greater demand for it, so it becomes more abundant in the economy. Lots of money flowing in an economy sounds like a good thing though, right? Wrong. Too much money supply results in inflation and inflation is basically the overall increase in goods and services. You pay more because your money is worth less. Retailers see this as an opportunity to increase the price of goods, so they can also get more from their money—it creates a pretty vicious cycle between buying and selling, and in the long term, it can be detrimental to any economy.

The US Federal Reserve Bank, for example, has the power to regulate inflation by adjusting the interest rate. The interest rate is the amount that a bank charges for using its money. A higher interest rate means it will be more expensive to take out a loan or pay. If you, however, purchased a bond or have your savings kept in a bank, you can earn an interest. It goes both ways. With great interest, comes great monetary value. This decreases demand, which effectively curbs overspending in the economy.

High interest rates equal greater value and low interest rates result in inflation and a low worth of money.

So, next time you pull out that £20 note, don't just look at Queen Elizabeth's face; appreciate the generations that created money for us to enjoy today.

Chapter 2:

The Backbone of Our

Financial System

Think about your car and all the components that work together to make it move. You have your engine, transmission system, front and rear axle, steering system, wheels, tyres, and brakes. If one of these don't work, the car could break down.

Similarly, that's how financial systems work.

The financial system is made of key institutions that enable the flow of money through the economy. It's held together by the basics of saving and investing. In this chapter, we'll be looking into *how* banks make money when you save and invest and how you make money through the same means. In this chapter, we'll look at bonds, the joint-stock companies, insurance, and the real estate market to understand our financial system.

In a nutshell, this is how the financial system works: In order for banks to make money, they need savers and borrowers. They work hand in hand and the bank is the middleman. When a saver, also known as a lender, deposits money into a bank, the bank will incentivize the saver by paying them in interest.

For example, the bank pays a lender an interest rate of 5%. The bank uses the lender's money to generate loans for a borrower. The borrower uses the loan to pay for a car, or a house or to start a business. The bank charges an interest rate on the loan, which the borrower has to pay back. The bank usually charges a greater interest rate for borrowers. In this example, we'll say 8%. The bank is effectively charging 8% and paying 5%, earning it an interest rate of 3%. The bank earns money from the borrowers' repayments and gives it back to savers when they withdraw money. It's a linear flow of money.

Lenders > banks > borrowers > loan paid back to the bank with interest > paid to the lender.

Banks lend out money at a higher interest rate than what they offered to savers, because that's how it makes its money.

This can also be compared to an economic system called the 'multiplier effect' whereby one purchase or economic activity paves the way for a string of economic activities to follow. It can either increase or decrease the growth of the economy. To illustrate the 'multiplier effect,' imagine a restaurant business.

1. The restaurant introduces a new chicken dish and it's the talk of the town.

2. It brings in more customers, therefore more sales.

3. This will lead to growth for the raw material suppliers (farms).

4. The activity in the agricultural industry will increase, having a positive effect on GDP.

5. The demand for more raw materials also means an increase in income for farmers or an increase in the number of farmers.

6. Employment increases.

7. The money paid to an employee is channelled back into the economy through various purchases, which could fuel the activity of another sector.

8. There is an overall increase in economic activity and growth.

9. Money deposited in the bank also grows by virtue of interest when savings and lending increases.

Growth = growth = growth = growth = multiplier effect.

Other than banks, the money can also flow through mutual funds, pension funds, investment banks and companies, real estate, insurance, and more.

What Is Credit and Debit?

Credit and debit are two sides of the same coin. One gives value (debit) and the other takes value (credit). Businesses balance their books by keeping record of their debits and credits—or the money coming in and the money leaving the account. They do this with the help of the double-entry bookkeeping system. It also ensures that nothing is amiss with the company's finances.

Inflow of money or debit orders increases assets or expense accounts and decreases liability, revenue, and equities. It appears on the left-hand side of the entry.

Outflow of money or credit increases liability and decreases asset or expense accounts. It appears on the right-hand side of the entry.

The accounting equation for debit and credit is Assets = Liabilities + Equity.

Assets are everything that the business owns from equipment, commercial vehicles, property and machinery, computers, and cash. They can be both tangible and intangible, like logos and trademarks. They give the business more value.

Liabilities are debts or money owed to other people, such as a business loan from a bank or other lenders, money owed to suppliers and to payroll taxes.

Equity is the owner's monetary interest in the business and it's the value payable to shareholders if the company were to be liquidated.

The History of Debit and Credit

Early forms of lending and borrowing dates back to 3,000 B.C. in ancient Mesopotamia, which we now know as the Middle East. People would use food to pay off their debts. Farmers, for example, would borrow seeds and use their harvest to pay off their debts.

The Code of Hammurabi, who was the sixth King of the First Babylonian Dynasty in 1792 B.C., created a collection of rules to establish the standards for commercial interactions. People used a debt-tablet, which was made out of clay, to record the debts owed. One rule cited in the Code of Hammurabi said if a borrower is unable to repay debts (in the form of food) due to climate or other reasons, they are allowed to 'wash-out' their debt-tablet, thus clearing them of making any payment entirely. Debt-tablets are similar to the modern day "I owe you."

This then advanced into a more structured form of keeping track of money paid and money owed. It was established in Italy by Venetian merchants during the Renaissance. It became known as the 'double-entry bookkeeping system.' It was developed by Italian mathematician Luca Pacioli, now revered as "The Father of Accounting." He wrote a book in 1494, which laid out the foundation for the system of debit and credit. It was established over 500 years ago and is a system still used around the world today.

Italy was the pioneer when it came to new finance and banking systems. During the Italian Renaissance, in the year 1397, Lorenzo de' Medici opened the first family banking system. The Medici family were prominent during the period, having lived in Florence, they had the influence and money to shape much of Italy's politics and financial system. Their influence spread throughout the world, and some of the Medici family's financial arrangements are still evident in the financial and banking sectors in Barcelona, Bruga, and other countries.

The Medici family were merchants during a time when trade was expanding throughout Europe. They used their political influence to acquire resources and loan their resources to other countries. They built most of their wealth through trade. Their banking system took their influence to even greater heights.

Here are three ways the Medici banking system is used today:

1. **The Double-Entry Bookkeeping System**

    Although this system was developed by Luca, as explained above, it was the Medici family that popularised it. The Medicis were wealthy, and the double-entry bookkeeping system helped them keep track of their finances and grow it at the same time. It also aided them in building a good and trusted relationship with traders and the country's people.

2. **Letter of Credit**

    A letter of credit is an agreement between two banks that guarantees payment from a buyer to a seller upon delivery of goods and services. Banks can cover the remaining cost in the event that a buyer cannot fully cover it. A letter of credit was an especially important mechanism for international trade and deals. One way that the Medicis capitalised from letters of credit is by claiming a percentage or fee when monies were transferred between banks. Credit helped create more money as we explained above.

3. **Holding Companies**

    The Medici family was also the first to model a modern holding company, further boosting their dominance in Europe. A holding company doesn't manufacture, sell, or conduct any business-like operations. Instead, it holds the controlling stock, assets, or interest of other companies, called their subsidiaries. They have the power to control the management and policies of its subsidiaries, including firing and hiring of managers and staff. The Medici's first holding company expanded across Milan, Venice, Rome, London, Barcelona, and more. Holding companies have a greater advantage over subsidiaries, in that, if a subsidiary goes bankrupt, the holding company will not be affected.

What Is the Bond Market?

A bond is an investment facility used to create money. Bonds are issued by the government to raise capital in order to fund infrastructure projects, and its growth is facilitated by interest rates. Publicly trading companies also issue bonds to fund expansion projects or sustain business operations. Bonds are a fixed-income investment, said to be more stable but with a low return.

During the Middle Ages, governments started issuing sovereign debts to fund wars. The Bank of England was the first and is the oldest central bank in the world established to raise money, by issuing bonds, to fund the British navy in the 17th Century. Banks in the US also started issuing treasury bonds to fund the military during two wars.

Bonds are basically tradable debt. When a government needs to raise money to fund new projects or pay off its own debts, it will sell bonds to investors. Bond holders earn an interest based on the face value of the bond they bought. Bonds are issued with a maturity date. Maturity is the number of years the bond holder keeps the bond while the bond-issuer raises money. At the end of maturity, the bond-issuer must repay the investor the original price of the bond.

For example, if a bond is purchased at £1,000 at face value with a 5% interest rate, the investor will receive £50 annually over the maturity period. Once the maturity period is over, the investor redeems his bond and the bank will return his principal investment, which in this example is £1,000. The bondholder also increased their profit off the interest earned.

Bonds are a low-risk investment option, and the only time you could lose your funds is if the issuer defaults on paying back the initial amount. Bonds with higher default risk have a higher interest rate, whereas bonds with a low default risk have a lower interest rate. Governments are seen as a more stable issuer of bonds, whereas businesses have a higher default risk, because they can go bankrupt. Overall, the interest payable to investors depends on the financial standing of the entity.

Bonds and Interest Rates

Bonds have an inverse relationship with interest rates.

When the interest rate rises, the price of your bond decreases, and when interest rates decrease, the price of your bond increases.

The price of the bond is fixed, and after it matures, the investor hopes to get the same money back on top of the interest earned annually. Take this, for example:

You purchase a bond for £20,000 with a fixed interest rate of 10% a year. This will earn you £2,000 a year. The interest rates in the economy increases to 15%, so bond holders will issue new bonds with this new interest rate. This means YOUR bond, compared to the new bonds with an interest rate of 15%, has less value. New bondholders will earn a greater profit on their bond and yours will be difficult to trade. The market becomes less competitive. You can, however, reduce the price of your bond to make up for the difference in interest rate.

If interest rates fall by 5%, then the value of your bond increases. That's because new bonds will be issued with the lower interest rate, earning investors a smaller profit. This will make the bond you have more valuable. You can even increase the face value of your bond to make it more attractive to other investors.

Bond prices are based on the basic law of supply and demand.

Supply increases when interest rates are low, and demand increases when interest rates are high.

As a bond holder, you would have to keep a close eye on the economy and especially the interest rates so that you can adjust the price of your bond to ensure you get the most profit out of it.

The Two Tiers of the Bond Market

There are two tiers in the bond market. A primary tier and a secondary tier. They work together to facilitate movement of money from savers to banks and other financial facilities.

The primary bond market is where the new bonds are generated and sold to investors to raise capital. Often referred to as 'the new issues' market. Transactions in the primary bond market take place between the bond issuer (government or corporate company) and the bond buyer (investor) directly.

The secondary bond market buys existing bonds (from the primary market) for reselling at a later stage. Investors therefore don't get bonds from the government or corporate, but from a broker instead. The broker is the middleman in this transaction. It facilitates the buying and selling between parties. Bonds in the secondary market can be resold in the form of a pension fund, mutual fund, life insurance policy, and other investment facilities.

There are five different bonds you can invest in: Government bonds, municipal bonds, corporate bonds, emerging market bonds, and mortgage-backed bonds (Hayes, 2019c).

Briefly, this is how they work.

- Government bonds, as we mentioned, are issued to help the state raise money to fund certain infrastructure projects or to pay for its own expenses. Interest is paid out to the bond buyer every year until the bond reaches maturity. Government bonds are the least risky, mainly because they are backed by the government, which can tax its citizens or print money to make repayments.

  The bonds issued by the US Government, for example, are known as Treasuries. You can either get a Treasury Bill, which is backed by the Treasury Department, with a maturity of one year or less. Then you get a Treasury note, which can be sold by the US Government on a fixed interest rate with a maturity of between one and ten years. Treasury bonds are the third option; they are issued by the US Federal Government and they have maturities of up to

20 years and more. Conservative investors usually chase after government bonds.

- Municipal bonds are locally issued by states, cities, special-purpose districts, public utility and school districts and other government owned entities which seek to raise cash to fund various projects. These bonds are tax-free or tax-exempted at state or local levels.

- Corporate bonds are issued by companies to raise money for its business operations, expansion plans and other expenses. Corporate bonds reach maturity in at least one year. Corporate bonds are, however, less stable, and high-risk because their return rate depends on the financial stability of the company.

Corporate bonds are rated in two ways.

1. Investment grade for high-quality bonds with medium to low risk.
2. Junk bonds or high-yield bonds with high returns but greater risk.

Junk bonds are more likely to default.

- Emerging market bonds are issued by governments and companies in emerging market economies. They offer great opportunities for growth to those economies but can also be unstable. This is thanks to the political and economic volatility of these nations. The rate of return on an emerging market bond, however, depends on that country's exchange rate as compared to your own. If the US dollar is weaker than the currency from that emerging market, it will have a positive effect on that bond.

- Mortgage-backed bonds relate to real estate and property. Investors who buy these bonds are essentially lending money to homebuyers through the bank. Returns are paid back on a monthly, quarterly, or semi-annually basis. We will look at real estate later on in this chapter.

What Are Joint-Stock Companies?

Let's say you're out for lunch with a friend. As you're looking at the menu, each of you finds a meal that you would like to eat, but you can't afford it. The meal costs £90. You only have £40, and your friend only has £50. Both of you can't afford to buy a plate of that meal individually, so you decide to put your money together and share the meal. Each of you gets a portion, thanks to the contribution you made.

That's kind of how a joint-stock company works, except instead of food, you're sharing a company with others. By definition, a joint-stock company is not owned by one single individual, but rather by several individuals called shareholders. Shareholders buy shares in the company, which helps the company raise cash, but at the same time gives the shareholder the power to make decisions about what happens in the company—they own a portion of it, after all. The degree of ownership depends on how many shares an investor buys.

Shares are transferable, but with limitations. In a public company, shares can be traded on registered stock exchanges, but shares of private companies are transferred subject to agreements between parties like family members etc.

Shareholders in a joint-stock company have unlimited liability. That means in the event a shareholder is unable to pay off debts, their personal belongings and property can be seized, especially if the company is in bad standing. Shareholders must bear the responsibilities for their privilege.

The History of the Joint-Stock Market

The idea for a joint-stock company originated in the 17th Century in Holland, what we now know as the Netherlands. It was developed in response to Spanish colonisers and Portuguese spice traders.

The Dutch were seafarers who would often trade spices in Asia, but at the time, the Portuguese had a monopoly on the spice trade, controlling all the trade routes to Asia and back. This made it difficult for the Dutch to continue their trade. They then decided to acquire spices from Lisbon in Portugal and ship them around Europe to sell and make a profit. Portugal was then absorbed into the Spanish empire, which resulted in the closure of the route to Lisbon. The Dutch then sought to sail all the way to Asia on their ships to acquire spices to keep their economy running. Shipping goods worked, until it didn't. Several ships carrying spices did not make it back to Dutch shores and those that did brought very little to the table.

The Dutch had to think of another plan, and they knew it had to be done together. Several expedition companies came together to form a single company, which held vast sovereign power. It was named the

United East India company, otherwise known to be the Verenigde Oost-Indische Compagnie (VOC). The establishment of the VOC would help the Dutch overturn their colonisers and build their own economy. The VOC also helped the Dutch take back its monopoly on the spice trade. The VOC started running low on money and couldn't carry out its planned operations. It then decided to set up a trading house in Amsterdam, called the Amsterdam Exchange Bank.

Dutch citizens were given the opportunity to buy shares of the company, helping the VOC raise the cash it needed. So ensued the first ever stock market and the first version of a joint-stock company.

The VOC itself had become the first publicly traded company in history. People from across Holland came to Amsterdam to trade, and in some cases even nationals from other countries. Holland had built itself its own empire, something that is still used today. Initially, the VOC raised over six million guilders, perhaps equivalent to about £110,000,000 today.

Joint-stock companies are founded on the virtue of 'stronger together.' When investors and individuals bring their money and resources together, more money can be raised and more can be achieved.

Joint-stock companies also emerged in Europe in the 13th Century. European colonisers sought to explore America in search of riches, but they were concerned about the accompanying risks, like travelling by sea. They were also reluctant to spend too much money on the expedition. The Europeans therefore had to make more money to fund their expeditions. This required expedition companies to come together and sell their shares to other investors, essentially funding their voyage into America. The new investors own a portion of the company and can also reap the rewards of the riches obtained.

When the company in question makes a handsome profit, shareholders receive substantial returns or dividends.

How Do Insurance Companies Work?

Ever heard those pesky adverts on radio calling on you to change your insurance for "better cover and lower premiums"? You're probably very familiar with the term 'insurance' and you know it's important to have it to protect your prized possessions, but how does it actually work? Often, financial advisors or insurance brokers guide us through the process, but it helps if you understand the process, too, because you never know if the guys in fancy suits are selling you the right product for a fair amount of money.

Insurance is a financial vehicle that helps spread risk to prevent financial ruin, or to cover losses in the event of an accident or natural disaster. It is a policy that an insurer sells to an individual in exchange for monthly premiums. The higher the risk, the higher the premium.

Say, for example, a client gets in a car accident, or their house gets damaged due to fire or flooding. The insurer will assess the situation and 'pay out' or reimburse their client. Before this, though, the insurer would have had to evaluate the property to create a policy for the client. The premiums paid act as a store of value. Having it in there in case of emergencies means you won't need to dip into your savings to pay for the damages, which could lead you into debt. Having an insurance policy simply gives you peace of mind.

Bottomry was perhaps the first form of insurance. It was a Maritime law that dates back 4,000–3,000 B.C. in Babylon. It is the arrangement between the master of a ship and the owner of the ship, which sought to 'cover' the ship in the event of damages.

When a master takes a ship out to sea, it takes a loan from the owner, pledging the ship itself as security to pay for the voyage. If the ship were to get damaged and needed to be repaired during a voyage, the ship master would need money, but they're out at sea, so they have no way of contacting the owner. This increases the risk of the ship suffering damage or worse, sinking. When this happens, the master of the ship is not obligated to repay the loan, the ship owner himself runs at a loss.

The bottomry contract became highly popular during the 15th Century. It was also recognized by the Ancient Romans, who then took it up a notch, creating the first version of life insurance. Burial societies in Rome paid for the funeral costs of its members out of monthly dues.

Life's risks and emergencies necessitated the need for insurance.

The Great Fire in London in 1666 gave rise to the first fire insurance company. This later became The Property Insurance Company. This is how it came to be:

The Great Fire of London broke out and damaged about 13,000 homes, St. Paul's Cathedral, parish churches, and other properties, most of which could not be recovered. People who were renting their home were liable for the damages and repairs, plus they had to continue paying rent while their homes were being rebuilt. The renters were already cash strapped. A 'Fire Court' was set up to sort this dispute, where the judge would decide who should rebuild and who should cancel their contracts on the premise of their financial abilities. This helped Londoners rebuild sooner rather than later.

This gave rise to other protection policies, including 'fire office,' said to be one of the first property insurance policies. More property insurance companies began to emerge. The London Assurance Corporation and the Royal Exchange Assurance Corporation are the most notable.

Lloyd's Coffee House

Around the year 1686 there was a little coffee shop in London called Lloyd's Coffee House, owned by Edward Lloyd. It was the prime location for merchant marine men, bankers, and traders to meet to get reliable information about shipping. The information was supplied by Lloyd himself. The information would later be published as 'Lloyd's list,' still in existence today.

The coffee shop was reorganised into a business, composed of underwriters and insurance brokers who would sell policies to clients.

For example, a sailor (the client) is looking to protect his ship from damage during voyage. So, he approaches an insurance broker, who will then evaluate the ship and determine its value vs its risks. In addition to that, the broker asks about the sailor's voyage, where he plans to set sail, and how much cargo is on the ship. The insurance broker, after evaluating value and risk, draws up an insurance policy for the client. The policy itself must first be evaluated by an underwriter, who removes a few risks and reduces the premium, or includes risks to increase the premium and cover. The lead underwriter makes major decisions when it comes to accepting the policy or other important decisions relating to claims. Once the policy is accepted, it becomes legal. The client pays an insurance premium—which is shared between the broker and underwriter. The ship's value is essentially covered.

In the worst-case scenario, the ship sinks, and the client needs to be reimbursed. The underwriter and the broker decide on an amount that is payable to the client as a claim settlement. The broker makes his money once the premium is paid. The underwriter has the option to reinsure the policy or transfer it to other underwriters, while retaining a share of the premium. This is how the underwriter makes money.

In modern day insurance, policies and money flow through Lloyd's of London and are reinsured or sold to other insurance firms. This spreads the risk for the client across a business community who each stand to earn profit from the premium or take a cut of every loss.

Insurance has evolved since, but the basic principle remains the same: It serves to prevent financial ruin by spreading risks.

When choosing an insurance policy, look at your own needs and budget and be cognizant of the three main elements:

Premiums: The monthly payment you make to the insurer to secure your cover. The amount you pay depends on your risk profile. If you live in a high-crime area, the premium of assets concerned, like your house or car, will increase.

Policy limit: This is the maximum amount that the insurer will pay under a policy for a covered loss. These are set per period, loss, or injury. Generally, a higher limit carries higher premiums.

Deductible: This is the specific policy amount the client must pay upfront before claiming their money from the insurer. A high deductible generally results in fewer small claims.

What Is the Property or Real Estate Market?

The real estate or property market has proven to be one of the most lucrative investment options, if not the largest. In 2019, at least 65.1% of American families owned their own primary residence, according to the Survey of Consumer Finances by the Federal Reserve.

The price of homes are known to steadily increase over years, earning the owner a hefty profit, but like every other investment option, growth depends heavily on the economy and movement within the market itself. Changes in interest rates have a significant influence on the price and value of property. It also gives investors a good indication on when to buy and sell property.

In a nutshell, when the interest rate is cut, there is a greater supply of properties, making it cheaper to get a mortgage. When interest rates increase, the demand for property increases, which in turn increases the price. Other factors that keep the real estate market moving are demographics, the economy, and government policies.

The History of the Housing Market in the US and UK

During the 20th Century, private property ownership was not a popular investment choice. Less than 10% of citizens in the UK owned their own property. About 100 years later, in the 21st Century, there was a property boom, which saw that 10% increase to 62%.

There are two types of privately owned property. One is freehold, which means both the land and the property belongs to a landlord. The other is leasehold, which means only the property on the land belongs to the owner, in other words, the property is rented out. When the leasing period is over, the land and property is returned to the landlord.

When you decide to buy a property that you don't have enough money for upfront, you take out a loan from the bank. In real estate terms, this is called a mortgage. A mortgage can be used to either purchase property or to pay for repairs and maintenance. Mortgages are paid back in installments, with interest. The property serves as collateral for the loan. If a property owner defaults on the loan, the bank can take the property.

Property owners who want to make money from their property instead of just paying back the mortgage can rent or lease the property. The money received as rent can then be used to help pay off the mortgage. At the same time, landlords can make a few extra pounds from these payments.

Although that sounds like a viable manner of paying off a property that's not being used, if things were to go wrong, like if the house suffers damage due to fire or other reasons, you as the sole owner of that property will be liable—unless, of course, you have insurance.

The US property market was marred with two great events: One, The Great Depression in the 1930s, and secondly, the financial crisis of 2008.

The stock market crash in 1929 was a result of a dwindling foreign stock market alongside an increase in borrowing from brokers to invest in stocks. The 1929 crash led to the downfall of the US economy that would take nearly ten years to recover. During this time, millions of Americans lost their jobs, businesses had to close down, property was lost, and many were left in a serious state of financial ruin.

The Dust Bowl was a severe drought in the southwestern Great Plains region of the United States, which had also inversely impacted the economy. In response, former US President, Franklin D. Roosevelt, established a 'New Deal' to lift the economy out of the doldrums. The New Deal was suggested so that the federal government had the ability to help the country out of the great depression. Under Roosevelt's leadership, banking reform laws, emergency relief programs, work relief programs, and agricultural programs were established. It, however, took the US economy and its housing market a long time to recover.

In the 2000s, the standards to get a mortgage were loosened, enabling more Americans to become homeowners. People who had low credit scores were able to qualify for low-cost, low-down payment mortgages, also known as subprime loans.

The subprime loans were packaged alongside high-quality loans and sold in bulk to institutional investors around the world. There was a huge demand for these packages, which gave rise to more foreign and domestic capital flowing into the US's mortgage-backed securities. More loans could be handed out as money flowed into the economy.

The loose structure encouraged more property sales, which helped lift prices. A whole lot more real estate investors entered the market. The market was in better standing so investors were able to obtain unlimited mortgages on investment property.

Conclusion

The decisions you make with your money have the power to move markets, sway supply and demand, influence trade decisions, and increase the overall growth in an economy.

The financial system needs YOU in order to make money. The multiplier effect is one way that this happens. Your daily economic activity has a ripple effect on the larger economy.

The other way you help the economy is by investing. Whether you choose to invest your money in bonds, joint-stock companies, the real estate market, or buy insurance, the economy will make more money.

Governments are then able to provide better infrastructure and services for the people. It helps businesses generate more money, and on top of all of that, it benefits you.

This also gives you, as a consumer, a greater variety on what you can spend your money on. Wanted that bicycle? It can be yours.

At the heart of it, the financial system was created in response to our needs and wants, our behaviours, and our general emotional instincts. If you go back to the first credit and debit transaction recorded, you will remember that it started off with food—a basic need.

The financial system also shows us the interconnectedness of humans. Aside from our investments benefitting us, you may have noticed that with you depositing money in a bank or by buying a bond, you're indirectly financially aiding another person seeking to take out a loan or a mortgage. They can use it to buy their dream home or start their business. You could be making someone's dreams come true, simply by investing.

This being the foundation of the creation of the entire financial system: working together. A company is nothing without the investor—if there's no one there to buy anything, a business just becomes a building, or an idea materialized that doesn't do anything.

As we read in the section on joint-stock companies, when more people come together and join their resources, more can be achieved. They say if you want to go fast, go alone, and if you want to go far, go together.

Chapter 3:

Wealth: A Definition

When was the last time you assessed your personal finances? How much money do you have in your current account and savings account? Do you have any assets or investments? How much are they worth? Against this, what are your monthly expenses, and have you been able to pay them comfortably?

It's important that you keep track of the money you've been accumulating in your accounts. Note down whether money has increased or decreased and note down why.

If your money has been increasing, despite your expenses, then give yourself a pat on the back. This means you're accumulating wealth.

- What Is Wealth?

Wealth, in general terms, means abundance. It can be applied to anything from your health, peace of mind, lifestyle, and more. For the purposes of this book, wealth is the abundance of money, both tangible and intangible.

When we talk about financial wealth, we look at all the savings, investments, and assets that a person or company may have accumulated over time. The true value of wealth is determined by net worth. Net worth is the wealth you are left with after your debts are paid. Wealth is basically the unchanging amount of money that you have saved or stored, that we hope to grow.

- **How Is Wealth Measured?**

People measure their wealth by subtracting their debt and expenses (not just monthly, but overall debt) from their accumulated savings and investments. Say, for example, you've been saving since your first paycheck. Two years down the line you have accumulated £150,000 (good on you) and so you decide to buy a car and pay it in installments over a course of four years, without interest. The car is valued at £60,000. If you were to take a snapshot of your current wealth status, your net worth is £90,000. You can then continue your savings journey by using your income to grow your wealth. We'll expand on this in the next chapter.

Businesses measure their wealth by looking at shareholders' equity or book value. Shareholders' equity is the *owner's claim* after subtracting total liabilities (debts) from total assets (what is owned). Book value is the company's net asset value after its liabilities are subtracted from its total assets. Book value is what *shareholders* will receive should the company go into liquidation.

Countries measure their wealth by looking at the total market value of the services and goods produced in the country during a period, usually annually. The official term for this is gross domestic product (GDP). When a country's GDP is high, the standard of living increases because the country has more money to provide better services and resources to its people. This can be in the form of better healthcare services, transport, high quality raw materials for food and clothing etc. The four main components that make up a country's GDP are:

1. Consumer Spending: This is the money that you, as an ordinary consumer, spend on your everyday basic needs and services. For example: Food shopping, clothing, car payments, or train fares. Your personal spending habits play a significant role in the country's GDP, because it reflects the needs and wants of the country through the patterns of supply and demand. If something, let's say coffee, is in high demand, then people are, firstly, willing to pay more for it. That's good for businesses overall. It also signals whether the country needs to produce more or import the commodity. In the broader scheme of things, you matter. In turn, when the economy performs well, consumers have more confidence in it, and end up spending more.

2. Government Spending: This is how the government spends money alongside what it invests in. Government expenditure goes towards maintaining the country's resources and services, infrastructure, equipment etc. Government spending also relies on the spending patterns of the consumer.

3. Investments or Business Capital: This is the money that businesses spend to improve their own operations. For example, a restaurant would spend more money on cooking equipment like ovens, stoves, crockery etc. What businesses buy is also an indicator of what the country needs in terms of production and resources. The more money businesses invest in themselves, the better it is for the country's GDP.

4. Net Exports: This is the difference between the country's exports (what it sells) and imports (what it buys). Using the coffee example: Ivory Coast is one of the world's largest coffee exporters because the commodity is abundant in the country, thanks to climate and other factors. Other countries will import or buy coffee beans from Ivory Coast and that sale would essentially boost its own GDP. The GDP of a country increases when it exports more than it imports.

- **Why Is it Important to Have Wealth?**

Having enough of something gives you a sense of independence. You don't have to rely on others, nor do you have to worry about when it will run out. Wealth does that for you. With enough money, that is not affected by how much you spend, you will be able to do what you need to: Go on holidays, buy the latest iPhone, start a business, or go to school. The world revolves around money and when you have enough of it, it makes living easier. Wealth is also about having financial security and peace of mind. Financial security is not something you have though, it's something you create. When you are financially secure, you have the freedom to do what you want, knowing you won't be left with a drained purse or bank account. That said, wealth does not flow. Instead, it grows.

- **How Do I Become Wealthy?**

By saving. There are only a lucky few people who were 'born rich' and who don't have to work a day in their lives. That's goals! You too, can be one of those people who doesn't have to work a 9–5 to become wealthy. You just need to learn to use your money better. Your 9–5 job does not equate to wealth. 'Making money' doesn't equate to wealth, but those things help you grow your wealth.

Wealth is considered to be a stock variable. Income is considered to be a flow variable. A flow variable is your income. It comes into your account, and it leaves your account through expenses and purchases. The value is constantly changing and the money moves. Wealth, on the other hand, is money that is kept as a store of value, meaning that it is money that you are holding, either in the form of a property, bonds, or machinery. It's something that helps you make more money—or become wealthy.

That said, wealth also increases when you save more and spend less. Let's go back to the car example: since purchasing your car, your net worth went from £150,000 to £90,000. This is okay, because you still have an income and that will help you sustain your lifestyle, but you also know that you would like to have that £150,000 staring at you every time you open your bank account. Aside from looking at other investment options (which we will look at in the next chapter), you decide you need to start saving more. To save more you need to spend less. Your income may not have changed, but if you want to save more money, you will have to adjust your spending habits. Maybe you stop buying lunch twice a week or resist the temptation to buy that new phone that's come out. Yours works just fine. Growing your wealth becomes your responsibility. As we said, money has power, but it is you who controls it.

- **Can Wealth Be Compared?**

Wealth is relative. You are only as wealthy as your community and society makes you to be. To be defined as a wealthy individual, you'd have to acquire assets that are scarce—this makes it a more prized possession and it makes you and your wealth stand out from the crowd. If everyone had the same amount of wealth, then our collective wealth would have no real value or a purpose. Wealth is not linear or standard. Each person or business places value on different things. For some it might be commodities: A coffee shop would value coffee more than it does alcohol, which a bar would value more. Each item has a different market value. Value is therefore defined differently.

We can, however, compare some factors between two businesses of similar nature. Take Mango and Zara, for example. Both have grown to become global brands, both are fast fashion clothing retailers, their offerings and their price range are similar. This makes them competitors. To stand out, one will have to either adopt a new strategy or produce goods that cannot be found elsewhere—this will make that retailer's products more valuable and prized, increasing its sales and wealth.

Money gives you power and power gives you control.

The same reason money has so much power over people is because it provides them with the same power.

As the famous author Joline Godfrey once said, "Money is just another word for power."

There are two sides to this coin.

Money gives you the power to influence people, it gives you agency, it gives you individuality and freedom. It gives you the power of choice. With enough money you can do what you want when you want. It pushes you further in life: You can start a business, continue your education, donate to charity, and help a friend in need. Money can also give you a higher status in society. Money means different things for different people—it depends on their needs.

The power associated with money can also lead to negative events like exploitation of people, assuming ownership over people, propaganda, greed, corruption, conflict, bribery, and assuming ownership of people. Wrong motives can lead you down the wrong path.

You get to choose how you can use that power.

Chapter 4:

How to Kickstart Your Wealth Creation

When you think about wealth creation, what is the first thing that comes to mind? Probably a big money balance in the bank? Maybe it's the image of Scrooge McDuck diving into a room full of gold coins.

The word 'wealth' means different things to different people. Often it depends on your needs and priorities, which depends on where you are in life. A university student is probably only looking for money to fund a social life and food. A father or mother might be saving to fund their child's education.

In Chapter 3, we looked at the definition of wealth, which in simple terms means an abundance. To measure your wealth, you would need to calculate your net worth. This is the money that remains after all your debts and expenses have been cleared. Wealth is a stock variable; it is fixed, unlike an income, which is a flow variable that is highly influenced by your immediate spending habits.

Wealth grows and you have the power to grow it. It all comes down to the financial decisions you make.

In this chapter, we will be exploring the different money-making options and mechanisms that exist. Most of these are founded on the financial system we explored in Chapter 2. As a reminder, five key institutions make up the financial system. These are: Credit and debit, bonds, joint-stock companies, insurance, and the real estate market.

The financial system has one key function, and that's to create money. Money is created with the help of lenders (people who save and invest) and borrowers (people who take out loans etc. from the bank). The bank benefits from the difference in interest between the lender and the borrower. Your participation in this cycle means you, too, have a lot to gain.

Bonds, as we explained, are issued by governments or companies to help raise cash to fund infrastructure projects or business expansion. Lenders earn an interest on the bond and get the principal amount back after it reaches maturity.

Investors are the glue that holds a joint-stock company together. As we explained, every individual's investment or contribution makes the company stronger. That means it will be able to achieve more.

Where insurance is concerned, you and your possessions are top priority. Insurance spreads risks to prevent financial ruin. It's only possible to spread risk when there are enough people participating in the insurance market. When more people are involved, the more money is accumulated, making it easier for you to claim your settlement in case there is an emergency.

The real estate market can only be possible with people who are willing to buy or willing to rent. We all need a place to stay, so at some point in your life, if you haven't already, you'll have to buy a house or rent or rent out your own house. The property market is stable, but economic downfalls, as we saw during the global financial crisis can adversely impact the price of houses. Interest rates are a very crucial determiner of the price of houses. Although the country's central bank makes the final decision, it is the people who influence it. The interest is adjusted when there is too little or too much money moving around in the economy. Adjusting the interest rate restores the value of money, giving you, the consumer, that much more buying power.

Your role is more important than you think. It's not that complicated to understand why.

Knowing how the financial system works gives you confidence to make your own financial decisions—that is the most important takeaway. Oftentimes people find that managing their finances is laborious and stressful, and this stems from the fear of making a mistake. Fair enough. That's why financial advisors exist. They offer guidance and advice on the different ways you can invest your money. It doesn't, however, come for free; there are some associated costs that you must pay if you decide to use a financial advisor. Which is okay, especially initially, but *Focused Financial Literacy, The Starting Point for Financial Success* seeks to empower you to learn how to do it yourself.

To become financially independent, you also need to become more independent. Trust yourself and your knowledge. You will make mistakes, but you will learn along the way.

The future is unpredictable, we never know what's going to happen tomorrow or in a year, and that's why it's important to have reserves or an emergency fund. The future can be less daunting when you know what to do, even when the world turns on you.

Emotional Maturity and Money

Our money-making decisions, foremost, come from our innate desires and instincts.

Maslow's Hierarchy of Needs was developed by Abraham Maslow, who was a specialist in human behavioural psychology. The hierarchy is an illustration that shows the connection between human needs and human desires. It is split into five categories.

- Physiological needs refer to our most basic needs and desires. These are the biological things that we need in order to survive. When our basic physiological needs are met, we are able to function better. They include food, water, oxygen, sex, and sleep—bathing and dressing falls under basic needs as well.

- Safety or security needs refers to what we need in order to feel comfortable and secure. When we are safe and secure, we are more capable. They include shelter (property), financial or job security, and health security.

- Social needs are the human and emotional connections we form with other people. It gives us a sense of belonging and community. We are social beings and need to interact with others. They include family, friends, and partners.

- Esteem needs refers to how we would like to be seen. It's our position in the world and how others see us. We want to feel loved and appreciated as humans. Our esteem needs are to be respected, to respect others, to have confidence, and a general sense of achievement.

- Self-actualization refers to our relationship with ourselves. It is in this space that we become more aware of ourselves, our desires, what we are capable of, our passions, and our purpose. Self-actualization means different things to different people but is the level that we are all striving for.

Maslow's Hierarchy of Needs shows how we as humans need our basic biological needs to be met before we can accomplish more in our lives. Once met, our needs slowly turn into desires.

Advertising companies base their marketing strategies on Maslow's Hierarchy of Needs. They target our needs and desires to sell their products and services to us. In that way, we can easily be influenced to buy things because it satisfies our instincts.

Marketing companies operate on the AIDA principle. It stands for:

A - attention

I - interest

D - desire

A- action

Advertisers employ the AIDA principle to create advertisements for us, the consumers. A successful advertisement will catch our **attention**, keep us **interested** or wanting to know more and how it will change our own lives, which brings on **desire** and when we desire something, we take **action** to obtain it.

Take clothing for example. It targets both our basic need to cover up as well as our esteem needs. Retailers know that we need clothes; they also know that wearing nice clothes or being trendy feeds into our confidence. They create advertisements that illustrate this. Think about how many advertisements, even billboards, you've seen of a trendy looking model getting attention or inviting love. Or think about how clothing retailers sell us 'a lifestyle.' We unintentionally internalise the life they are selling to us, and if we are not aware, our desires will override our logic and we'll go on a spending spree.

Online shopping is also booming, making it even easier for us to make a quick and impulsive buy, plus, when you don't physically see the money leaving your wallet, you tend to pay more. There's a trick to avoid impulsive online shopping. Here's how it works:

If while shopping online, you find something you would like to buy immediately, don't. Don't buy it. Put it in your basket and leave it there for about a day or two. If after the waiting period, you feel that you can do without it, you have passed the test. Empty your basket and do that whenever you feel like buying like crazy.

If your intention is to make money and create wealth, you must garner willpower to walk away from temptation. The world preys on your emotions, but emotions too, are something you can control. If you can control your emotions or be mindful when deciding, you can control your money. If you allow your emotions to help you make financial decisions, then you risk making tiny mistakes here and there which will eventually amount to huge losses. When it comes to saving, think about how your current behaviors will affect your future. Does it look good? If not, then what adjustments can you make?

Before you start investing, you need to identify your personal needs, priorities, and financial goals. You can start by asking yourself these five important questions.

1. What are my financial needs?
2. How much do I need to cover my basic financial needs?
3. What changes can I make right now to save and spend better?
4. What are my short-term financial goals?
5. What are my long-term financial goals?

Be honest with yourself and also be practical. Building wealth does not happen overnight. At times, you may only reap the rewards of your investments after some years, and it's also important to note that there will be times where you will lose money. Investing in itself is a gamble. Sometimes you win and sometimes you lose, but the more familiar you are with the financial system and its inner workings, the more likely you are to win every time. That's absolutely possible.

Once you have identified your basic financial needs and goals, you can start working on them. Ideally, you should be consistent with your saving habits, but we all know mistakes can happen along the way. Remind yourself what is important. It is advisable to create a list of your financial priorities and keep it handy, look at it whenever you feel like you are straying from your intentions. Whenever you feel like making an impulsive purchase, look at your list and see if it aligns. We're not saying you're not allowed to spoil yourself once in a while: the little spending rewards are encouraging but at the same time, covering your main expenses first gives you peace of mind, and that's something money can't buy.

Feeling inspired yet? Then let's kickstart your wealth creation.

What Is Compound Interest?

There are two methods of earning interest on an account. One is simple interest, and the other is compound interest.

First, the basics: Interest is what the bank pays you for saving your money. It's basically a reward for lending.

Simple interest is a straightforward formula whereby the money you invested in a bank grows according to a fixed interest rate, either yearly or monthly. Your earnings won't change significantly over each time period. Say, for example, you deposited £1,000 into the bank with a yearly interest of 5%. At the end of the year, you would have made an extra £5, bringing your total at the end of year one to £1,050.

Compound interest is a little complex, but it's worth understanding. It was thought to have originated in 17th Century Italy. In financial terms, the word 'compounding' essentially means to make more of or to combine a few things to make a 'whole.' It can also be referred to as 'stacking' things. If you look at the word 'compound' in that context, it makes it easier for you to understand its function.

By definition, compound interest is the interest earned on money that has been accrued by interest. Your investment generates earnings, and then those earnings generate their own earnings through interest.

The interest rate is usually fixed, but your earnings change according to how much you already have saved.

Let's break it down using the example of £1,000 at a yearly interest rate of 5%.

Initial payment: £1,000 with 5% interest

At the end of year one, you collect £50 = £1,050

At the end of year two, you collect £52.50 = £1,102.50

At the end of year three, you collect £55.13 = £1,157.63

At the end of year four, you collect £57.88 = £1,215.51

At the end of year five, you collect £60.78 = £1,276.28

At the end of year ten, you would have collected £77.57 = £1,628.89

At the end of year twenty, you would have collected £126.35 = £2,653.30

In the long-term your savings will be influenced by five key factors. These are:

- Frequency: Your earnings will increase if your compounding periods are more frequent. If you earn interest on a daily or monthly basis, rather than a yearly basis, your money will grow much faster. It is advisable to look for accounts with a daily compounding period—you will see a huge difference at the end of the month.

- Time: It takes time for the money to grow, so be patient. Leaving your money untouched in an account for a long period of time will reap rewards.

- Interest rate: The higher the interest rate, the faster you will earn money. Lower interest rates in a compound account will still earn you more overtime than high interest rates in a simple interest account.

- Deposits: Try to avoid withdrawing money as much as you can, doing so will break the momentum of the on-interest earnings of a compound interest account. Depositing money will boost your earnings.

- Starting amount: The amount of money you initially put down won't change compounding. You will still earn money, it may just seem bigger when you start off with a bigger amount, but the pace stays the same—it all mostly depends on rate and time frame.

Compound interest favours you if you're a saver or lender, but it can work against you if you're borrowing or taking out a loan, because you will have to make repayments with interest—essentially paying back more than you loaned.

It was Albert Einstein who once said, "compound interest is the eighth wonder of the world." He also said that those who understand it, earn it, and those who don't, pay it.

Here's how you can make compound interest work for you:

- Start saving early and save often

The earlier you start saving money, the better. You will accumulate more over a fixed period of time. The more money you save, the faster your money will grow. What you put in is what you get out.

- Choose the right investing facility

Banks often publish their annual percentage yield (APY), which is the real rate of return earned on a savings or investment account. Compare products offered by different banks to get more out of your savings. Since you're new to this, a bank is a safer option than investing in a stock.

- Pay off debts

To avoid getting on the bad side of credit, pay off any outstanding loans and debts sooner rather than later. You don't have to pay it all off at once, but starting will at least pay the interest, as it accrues. It's like a pothole—the longer you leave it, the larger the gap will become. You will save yourself from paying a large sum in the future.

- Avoid borrowing

If you want to make more money, you have to spend less or spend less on things that you can't afford. Expensive purchases can lead you down a dark road of debt, with the risk of increasing your credit. This will only make it all the more difficult for you to pay back the money. This goes for huge purchases like a car or small purchases like an expensive clothing item. Save more than you spend, and when you spend, spend wisely.

Investment Fees and Costs

It costs money to *make* money. A lot of investment options out there are accompanied by a fee, which is usually paid to the company and the broker involved.

Seeking advice from a broker is pretty practical, especially if you're new to investing. A broker can show you the ropes and guide you in the right direction. At the same time, however, having a broker can leave a dent in your wallet without you even realising it.

There are many hidden fees behind the scenes of investing, and if you're not careful enough, you could end up spending more on fees than you are on saving and creating wealth.

That being said, there are three key terms you need to be aware of when looking for an investment vehicle and also when choosing a financial advisor.

1. Loaded Funds / Sales Load

This is the kind of investment option that you have to pay to invest in. Your fee is paid to an intermediary, such as a financial planner, financial advisor, or broker for their time and for advising you on the different investment options available to you. The load/payment is either made at the time of purchase (front end), when the shares are sold (back end), or for as long as the fund is held by the investor. This is one type of a mutual fund, another is a 'no-load fund,' meaning that you will not be required to pay the broker or financial planner.

All the money invested in a no-load fund is for the investor only. So, if you purchased £10,000 worth of a no-load fund, the full £10,000 will be invested. Where a loaded fund is concerned, the investor will have less than the initial amount to invest, because a percentage will go to the broker. That percentage depends on the class of the mutual fund.

A mutual fund is made up of a pool of money from many investors looking to put their money into securities like stocks, bonds, money market instruments, and other assets.

2. Expense Ratio

This is a percentage of your investment that goes towards the management of the fund itself. It is also referred to as 'management expense ratio.' The expense ratio can also be also expressed as the mutual fund operating costs relative to assets. Expense ratios help the investor decide if the fund is worth investing in given its fees. Ideally, expense ratios should be between 0.5% to 0.75% for the investor. Anything above 1.5% is considered a high expense ratio. Generally, bonds and international funds do have a high expense ratio, they also tend to have higher returns, but if you're looking to minimise fees, then go for an investment option with a lower expense ratio, such as stock index funds.

3. Commissions

This is what the financial advisor or broker will charge you for advising you on investment options or for handling purchases and transactions. Some financial advisors charge a flat rate for managing a client's work, and they are known as fee-based advisors.

Financial advisors basically profit from your lack of understanding of the financial system and the investment market, therefore, if you are using a financial advisor, it is crucial that you ask about the hidden costs and fees behind every transaction and every sale. By law, financial planners are expected to disclose all hidden clauses to the client. Most financial advisors are honest about the fees and do have your best interests at heart, but there will also be some rotten tomatoes of the lot. Also be wary of the 'top financial advisor.' Note that they are the ones that bring more profit into the company and often that comes off YOUR fees. Clarify their position and strategy, then decide if you can work with them.

Where possible, avoid paying commissions; it helps if you research everything before so you can ask the right questions and not blindly follow your financial planner. At the same time, don't avoid commissions at the expense of higher expense ratios.

Here's an example courtesy of The College Investor (Farrington, 2017):

"If you have a commission-free fund at 0.10% expense ratio, and an ETF that you'll pay £4.95 for, but has just a 0.06% expense ratio—go with the lower expense ratio. Since it's a percentage of your investment, that's more money than any commission! But note, as of 2020, most brokerages are commission-free for ETFs anyway.

In this example if we invested £20,000—the expense ratio at 0.10% is £20. At 0.06%, it's £12 per year—a savings of £8 per year—already overcoming the commission expense of just £4.95."

On that note, don't be too disheartened by the fees and costs associated with investing. Remember that the financial system is built on mutual trust and coming together. Your money helps keep some of these institutions running. You just have to be mindful about where you're putting your money and what you intend to get out of it.

What Financial Products Are Out There?

From company stocks to government bonds, securities, cash, and exchange-traded funds. There are hundreds, if not thousands of investment options available to you, giving you an even greater opportunity to increase your wealth.

Financial experts often talk about diversifying your investment portfolio, that means to put your money in several different investments, to spread your risk. If you invest all your money in just one portfolio, you risk losing it all if the market goes bad and your stock is affected. That's why they say, 'don't put all your eggs in one basket.'

When it comes to investing, you will never know if you're making the right choice until you make the choice. Investing is gambling, but with a strategy. Markets can change at any moment, as we saw when Covid-19 struck the world, but to stay prepared and to go with the flow, know *how* to choose an investment and how to secure the right price for them.

Choosing how and where to put your money also plays a role in how much wealth you can accumulate. You can have a mix between traditional investment facilities like your bonds and stocks and then some alternative investment options like venture capitals, hedge funds, and even art.

The advent of technology has also made it much easier to access different types of investment vehicles, some with a financial advisor and other online ones that completely cut out the middleman. If you want, you can also get help from a robo-advisor.

A 'robo-advisor' is exactly what it sounds like. It's an automated, algorithm-driven, financial planning tool that helps you make financial decisions. No humans are involved in the process. The robo-advisor collects information about the client's financial goals and their current financial situation. It assesses the information and presents financial planning options that the client can employ. Pretty nifty.

Some of the services offered by a robo-advisor include a comprehensive goal-oriented financial plan, account services, advice on how to manage your portfolio, on the ball customer service and financial education. They're low cost, secure, and easy to set up.

Here are some top picks for every kind of investor, courtesy of Investopedia (Carey, 2020).

- Wealthfront: Top rated and best for setting goals

- Interactive Advisors: Best for socially responsible investing and portfolio construction

- Betterment: Best for beginners and cash management

- Personal Capital: Best for portfolio management

- M1 Finance: Best for sophisticated investors and low costs

- Merrill Guided Investing: Best for education

- E*TRADE Core Portfolios: Best for mobile

Alternative investment options are booming and it's giving investors more freedom and choice with what they would like to do with their money. Maybe bonds are not really your thing but investing in a venture capital would interest you. Venture capital, or in short, VC, is a private equity investment option for those looking to provide money to small businesses and start-ups. It may be a risky option because start-ups do have teething problems and some never really take off. It is therefore up to you to decide if a particular venture capital resonates with you.

Cryptocurrency is another fascinating example of an alternative investment. Cryptocurrency is gaining a lot of traction as an investment. However, it's a volatile landscape and definitely not a get-rich-quick formula. If you are keen to try investing in crypto, it's a good idea to build your wealth foundation in the other asset classes outlined in this chapter first and then try your hand at cryptocurrency investing.

Alternative investments options are riskier than your traditional bonds, stocks, and cash, because they are still emerging. Due to the nature of the alternative investments, mostly high-net worth individuals invest their money in it. Alternative investments are also not regulated, so the information published on them may not be completely accurate.

The interesting thing about alternative investments is that most of it cannot be converted into cash. That's because it's not easy to put a price on something irreplaceable, like a collectible, a piece of art or a vintage bottle of wine. Additionally, not everyone will want it.

Investing online has also taken off. You can now invest using apps. Here are five apps that let you invest for free (Farrington, 2020).

- M1 Finance - Building a free long-term portfolio for the long-term.

- Fidelity - Full service investing at £0 trade prices.

- TD Ameritrade - Free options trading.

- Robinhood - 100% Free stock trades & limited crypto.

- Vanguard - Low-cost index fund investing.

Your investment choices are unlimited and as the world changes, more investment options will appear. Just as the investment market grows, so will your financial reach and only you have the power to choose how you want to make money. Continue reading and asking questions about the markets, the economy, and how things work. There's something new to learn every day. Your only limitation is yourself. Go out there!

The World of Finance

Think back to ten years ago. Social media was only emerging. Facebook was only a few years old, and smartphones weren't mainstream. For the most part, we still used phones that had buttons on them, and we had no idea how to take a selfie.

Technology is changing. If you think back, most people joined Facebook to keep in touch with old friends and family. Now, Facebook is a platform where you can buy and sell stuff, find a job, and even advertise your business—for free. Facebook is so much more than just a place to keep in touch with people you know.

Instagram, too, was once just a picture-sharing platform. Now targeted advertisements appear on your feed, with the option to go directly to the website to buy things. Businesses are letting go of traditional methods of advertising. Pamphlets and posters are no longer effective and with Netflix and other streaming platforms, no one really watches TV anymore. These are not the only ones: TikTok is fairly new, Snapchat grew in popularity when it came up with new features like filters—who knew we could make ourselves look like a dog? It also had a feature to share a picture that would only be visible for a short while. Facebook, Instagram, and Twitter now have the same feature. They integrated it with their primary purposes, giving them greater functionality and reach. Snapchat didn't adapt as quickly and got left behind.

This is the fourth industrial revolution, and we can expect to see huge changes in the way we live our lives, the way we work, and the way we make money. The world is becoming more aware of global inequality, human rights, and climate change. Social media is being used as a space to create awareness, start campaigns, and even crowdfund for causes.

As the world changes, we need to learn how to do things differently.

Think about climate change. It has become a huge issue in our world today. With more people advocating for clean energy and sustainable living, energy companies across the globe are at risk of collapse. On the other hand, some energy companies are changing their strategies to reduce harmful emissions and seek alternatives like renewable energy. In recent years, there's been a boom in the solar panel industry as people seek to reduce electricity that is generated from burning coal. Electric vehicles are also growing in popularity, which means traditional cars running on petrol could be phased out.

The UK has made a pledge to reduce its carbon emissions by 78% by the year 2035 (Gov.UK, 2021).

It plans to do this by supporting the rollout of more electric vehicles, low-carbon heating, renewable energy, and reducing meat and dairy consumption. The UK Government has also encouraged people to drive less and walk or cycle more. It also plans to increase the price of aviation to reduce frequent travellers from using planes.

Take a step back and think about all the businesses, manufacturers, and suppliers that would be affected by these changes.

Take the meat and dairy industry, for example. If the consumption of these products is reduced, then cattle farmers (the producer of raw materials) will suffer a loss; so will the meat suppliers, butcheries, and even restaurants.

If those restaurants sold stocks, then that too will be in low demand, further hurting the business. The entire supply chain gets affected. So, businesses had to think fast. Now we have plant-based burgers that contain no meat products but can to some level alleviate pressure on the food industry.

We know that the economy is made up of three main sectors, namely: The primary, secondary, and tertiary.

The primary sector is concerned with the raw materials that are extracted from the earth, such as grain, cotton, fisheries, wheat, coal, minerals, and more.

The secondary sector has to do with production and manufacturing. This is where the raw materials from the primary sector are transformed into something that we can consume, wear, or use, like a car or machinery.

The tertiary sector is where goods produced in the secondary sector are packaged and sold to customers and businesses. The tertiary sector also provides commercial services to the general population as well as businesses.

When people purchase these goods and services, they inject more money into the economy. An abundance of resources would make their price low, increasing demand and perhaps increasing the amount of money moving about in the economy. When money supply increases, so does the cost of living. This is inflation. Money in high supply has less value. To increase the value of money, the Bank of England will jump in to regulate the fluctuations. It does this by increasing the interest rate. This will reduce demand for money. The interest rate also ties back to your investments.

The higher the interest rate, the greater your earnings on some investments, for example, bonds or real estate.

In 2020, a global pandemic struck the world. It goes by the name of Covid-19. Countries throughout the world imposed strict lockdowns to prevent the spread of the virus. Restrictions differed from country to country, but in most, businesses were forced to shut down for a while. Some businesses survived the lockdown, others had to sadly close forever. Sales and economic productivity decreased, people lost their jobs, and economies across the world suffered. In 2020 the US's GDP contracted by 2.3%, after increasing 4% in 2019 (bea.gov, 2021). With everything coming to a standstill, money could not flow through the economy, and this affected every industry, from mining to clothing retailers, factories, and even some huge corporations had to let go of staff. The pandemic affected anyone and everyone.

The pandemic caused a disruptive ripple effect across the world, and it will take years before the global economy recovers. That said, we can see how the many factors in the economy come together to ensure there is a constant flow of money. When the economy comes to a standstill, lots of things can change in a day. This has also forced companies to reassess their business strategies to adapt to this 'new normal' to ramp up sales and productivity.

The pandemic gave rise to a new economic dynamic that many businesses are still trying to figure out. If there was one lesson that the pandemic taught us, it's that things can change in an instant. That's why it's important to think ahead, especially when it comes to saving money.

The ABCs of Wealth Creation

In Chapter 3, we looked at the definition of wealth. Just to recap, wealth is the money that remains after your debts and expenses are fully paid off. Wealth is a stock variable, unlike income, which is a flow variable. Wealth remains.

Once you start accumulating wealth, you can trust that it will only grow with time and consistent saving.

The question, however, is where does wealth come from?

The moment money enters your wallet or bank account for the first time is the moment you own wealth.

That money can come in the form of pocket money when you were a teenager or from your income as an adult. Wealth doesn't necessarily have to mean millions of pounds. It simply means you own more than you need to spend during that particular time.

Having wealth is one thing, but life moves, and when life moves, so do the needs and expenses. The wealth you accumulated at 18 won't fund your lifestyle at 30. That's why you need to change your spending habits to grow your money.

First you need to identify your financial goals.

- Are you saving for something specific like a house, car, or holiday?

- How much money would you like to accumulate after 10 or 15 years?

- Do you know how to achieve these financial goals?

The Richest Man in Babylon by George S Clason provided 'seven cures for a lean purse' (Clason, 1926). They are:

1. Save money.

2. Don't spend more than you need.

3. Multiply your wealth—invest wisely.

4. Avoid investments that sound too good to be true.

5. Own property.

6. Protect yourself with life insurance.

7. Learn more about investing and finance.

To build on the above, there are three key things that you need to do to build your wealth. Let's call it the ABCs of wealth creation.

A. Pay Yourself First

"For every ten coins thou placest within thy purse take out for use but nine. Thy purse will start to fatten at once, and its increasing weight will feel good in thy hand and bring satisfaction to thy soul."

Channel your main source of income into your savings first. Do not spend money the moment you receive it, get into the habit of saving first, spending second. Clason suggests you set aside 10% of your salary and put it away into a savings account. Consistency is key when it comes to saving. Do it as often as you can.

B. Keep Your Expenses Low

"What each of us calls our 'necessary expenses' will always grow to equal our incomes unless we protest to the contrary...Confuse not the necessary expenses with thy desires...Study thoughtfully thy accustomed habits of living. Herein may be most often found certain accepted expenses that may wisely be reduced or eliminated."

Track your expenses. Take note of any expense that you can cut; maybe it's that monthly magazine subscription or a gym membership that you no longer use. The less money you spend, the more you can channel towards your savings. Make every pound count.

C. Invest What You Save

"Make thy gold multiply."

"The gold we may retain from our earnings is but the start. The earnings it will make shall build our fortunes...To put each coin to labouring that it may reproduce its kind... a stream of wealth that shall flow constantly into thy purse...an income that continueth to come whether thou work or travel."

Invest the money that you have saved so far in a compound interest account. Your savings will multiply year on year. If you leave it to grow, your wealth will exceed your expenses and debts, and you can then spend a little more comfortably.

Here are seven more tips from Clason to inspire your wealth creation journey:

- To bring your dreams and desires to fulfillment, you must be successful with money.

- "A man's wealth is not in the coins in his purse. It is in his income."

- You will only begin building wealth when you start to realise that a part of all the money you earn is yours to keep. That is, pay yourself first. You always pay others for goods and services. Pay yourself as much as you can.

- The more we know, the more we may earn. The person who seeks to know more of their craft is capable of earning more.

- If you are in debt, live on 70% of what you make. Save 10% for yourself. Use the remaining 20% to repay your debts.

- Stick with the plan. Money accrues surprisingly quickly, and debts are gone fast with discipline and consistency.

- Do not live beyond your means (Clear, n.d.).

Passive vs Active Income

Passive income or residual income is what you get when you leave your money to grow in your accounts. It's everything we've talked about until now. Passive income supplements your active income. It's the money you accumulate off interest in your savings and investments, or in some cases rental income or dividends. You don't have to do much to earn a passive income, except to let it grow. Passive income is essentially what grows our wealth.

Passive income is earned over the long-term, so be patient. Passive income is basically money you are growing to use in the future—but if you don't have a stable salary, then you need to learn how to properly ration your money. But if you can help it, don't frequently dip into your passive income accounts, rather use cash reserves or money that you have saved in a cash account. These are meant for short-term savings.

Tracker funds/index funds is another method of earning a passive income. Index funds were designed to expose investors to a pool of securities in a market index at low-cost. Index funds seek to replicate performance of the market index. Investors can also customise their own index funds for more targeted investments.

If your passive income is spread across a number of portfolios, it might be difficult to track the movements in each account. Plus, it will save you from getting into trouble with the tax man. Yes, passive income is taxable.

Here are six things you can do to track your passive income (Bondigas, n.d.).

- Treat it Like a Business

In a business, money flows in and money flows out. The same thing applies to how you manage your passive income. Keeping it separate from your fixed-job income also helps, as you'll take note of how much money is flowing in and how much is flowing out. Use this time to also see the performance of your passive income accounts.

- Know How Taxes Work

Your passive income can't escape taxes. Learn about your HMRC obligations and how it affects your income. You may need to file quarterly income estimates and pay taxes then. However, you might get deductions for equipment you buy for running your passive-income business. Keeping business and personal bank accounts separate helps facilitate this (Bondigas, n.d.).

- Separate From Personal

Don't merge your active income account with your passive income account. Keeping all your money in one place is risky. If an account were to be hacked, all your money would go. You can save all your residual income in one place, like a PayPal account. If you find an online bank that pays interest, then that's even better, because you'll be earning on top of what you have already earned. You should link your personal account to your online account, so every so often you can 'pay yourself.' If you have more than one passive income stream, then keep a separate account for each.

- Use Accounting

You can use a spreadsheet, online tools, or even an old-fashioned ledger to track your income. Log each income item as you receive it, plus other details like where you got it from. It can be rent, investment income, or from book royalties. Alternatively, if this seems like too much work, consider online tools that do it for you automatically. The key though, again, is to keep accounts separate.

- Account Analytics

While you're tracking your money flowing into and out of your account, you might also want to have a look at the performance of your investment accounts. Check if there's been any significant changes and if you need to do anything about it. Don't obsess over it, though. If you keep looking, it will seem like nothing has changed, but over time, seeing a big number will give you a sense of gratification.

- Pay Yourself First

If you don't have a full-time job with a stable income and your passive income is the only one you have, then, you will need to pay yourself a salary. Figure out how much money you need every month and transfer it into a current account. Budgeting is crucial for this. You don't want to keep using your passive income—you have to keep saving.

Saving to create a passive income account has to start somewhere, right? That's why we have active income. This is the opposite of passive income in the sense that you have to actively be doing something to earn it. It's either a job or a side-gig or anything that debits your account every few weeks. Active income is earned more consistently. It's easier to access and manage because it's all in one place.

These two forms of earning income are opposite, but they can work hand in hand. As we explained, you need money from your active earnings to accelerate growth in your passive earnings. If you don't have a 9–5 job with a stable salary, then your passive income basically becomes a full-time job. You should use this time to learn more about the market, different securities, and options you can invest in.

If your goal is to make more money fast, then you need to be consistent with the way you manage your money. You can spread your income across your investment accounts and portfolios, especially when the market is looking good, to get more from your bucks.

Alternative saving accounts, which we spoke about earlier in this chapter, is another way you can accelerate growth in your investments. As we explained, alternative savings are those that move away from the traditional bonds, stocks, and cash.

In the UK, an Individual Savings Account (ISA) is a type of alternative savings account. ISAs are tax-free, so your earnings from either cash or investment gains are not taxed. This essentially means you can retain more money. Due to the generous tax-breaks, there's a limit to how much money you can invest in an ISA each year. The amount can change every year. These yearly deposits are called ISA allowances.

Remember the 10% of income that you were to put aside to pay yourself? This is a good place to put it. You can choose one of the four options below to start saving tax-free.

- Stocks and Shares ISAs: These let you invest your ISA allowance in the stock market, potentially increasing your earnings in the long term. Stocks are volatile though, so you can lose money.

- Cash ISAs: Your money is invested with a fixed interest rate over a set period of time and your income is guaranteed.

- Junior ISAs: Junior ISAs will kickstart your child's savings and wealth.

- Lifetime ISAs: The government adds a 25% bonus to the money you invested until you hit 50. You can use the money to buy your home or fund your retirement. You will be charged 25% on any money that you withdraw.

The US provides a number of different tax-free savings accounts (TFSAs), where capital gains and returns are not taxed, making it easier and faster (thanks to compound interest) to save for your long-term and short-term goals. These can range from school fees, a down payment on a house, or a holiday. Banks, credit unions, insurance companies, and trust companies can issue tax-free savings accounts. It is advisable to go for an insured institution to open your tax-free savings account, so your money is more secure.

To ensure optimum results when saving and investing your money, your accounts should consider the following:

Outperform inflation: Your savings and investments must be protected from fluctuating inflation—accounts that don't respond to inflation maintain their value for longer. Some examples of anti-inflation investments include assets like gold, commodities, real estate investments, and treasury inflation protected securities (TIPS). There's a variety of other stocks that can beat inflation.

Geographically diversified: Don't limit yourself to financial services and investments in your own country. Spread your risk and stretch your pound by locking away some money in the stocks of other countries. Countries with high GDP and a stable economy with vast resources to leverage off are ideal for investment. Here are the top ten countries you should consider investing in (The Best Countries to Invest In, 2021). Please note, the list below is an example only and can change dramatically over time:

1. Mexico with a GDP of £1.27 trillion
2. Indonesia with a GDP of £1.12 million
3. Lithuania with a GDP of £54.6 billion

4. United Arab Emirates with a GDP of £421 billion
5. Malaysia with a GDP of £365 billion
6. Portugal with a GDP of £239 billion
7. Switzerland with a GDP of £703 billion
8. Croatia with a GDP of £60.8 billion
9. Poland with a GDP of £596 billion
10. Brazil with a GDP of £1.84 trillion

Diversify financial products: Mixing up your investments between traditional forms like cash, bonds and stocks, along with alternative investments like your TFSA and some digital investment options will not only reduce your risk but will grow your money at different rates. If you put all your money in one account, you could risk losing it all if things go bad for that business or stock. As we said above, 'don't put all your eggs in one basket.'

How Do I Start Investing?

Begin with asking yourself these two crucial questions:

1) How safe will my money be if I invest it into this product?
2) How much can I expect in returns?

Investment Products

There are thousands of different products that you can invest in. Here are the main ones, plus their advantages and disadvantages.

1. Cash Investments

These are for investors looking for a short-term investment vehicle. Investors preserve their cash in these accounts while looking for other more lucrative investment options.

Cash investments are low risk and stable but offer low returns on interest.

You can invest your cash in either a savings account, a money market account, or a certificate of deposit (CD).

Money market accounts have slightly higher interest rate returns compared to cash savings accounts. Money market accounts are liquid investments that pay variable interest returns, while a CD is similar to a bond. The investor earns interest in intervals, funds are, however, locked in the bank, and withdrawing it will incur a penalty unless the CD is held with a brokerage.

2. Bonds

Investors can buy bonds from the government and companies that are trying to raise capital. Interest is fixed for the period of maturity, thereafter the principal amount is paid back to the investor. There are several types of bonds you can invest in.

Returns on a bond are fixed, they have low-risk and low-volatility, but they are less liquid and directly impacted by interest rates.

3. Shares, Stocks, and Equities

Stocks, shares, and equities are different names for the same thing. A stock is a short or long-term investment in an individual company. Investors buy shares or stocks from a company in exchange for an annual or biannual dividend. When choosing which stock to buy, rather focus on companies with strong annual earnings or growth.

Stocks have a high return but are also high risk. The value of stocks are pegged to the performance of the company.

4. Funds

Funds are pools of capital that are supplied by several investors, who then use the funds to collectively purchase securities. Each investor retains control and ownership of their own shares. The different types of investment funds include mutual funds, exchange traded funds, money market funds and others. Funds are usually managed by fund managers and offer an option to reinvest but they can be high in fees. Although, you should take note of who the fund manager is, as this also influences your funds. Mutual funds and ETFs are good for diversification in your portfolio because they are composed of several other stocks and other investments, which increase their inherent value.

5. Commodities

Commodities are anything from raw materials from the earth, such as metals and minerals, oil, and agriculture. You can purchase a commodity directly or indirectly. A direct purchase means you buy actual gold or minerals that you can resell. Or you can buy it through stocks in a company. Commodities help diversify your portfolio. They are tied to inflation, so prices move together. Your earnings are based on the price of the commodity which makes it very volatile.

6. Insurance Products

When you purchase insurance, you are basically purchasing protection for something you own like your car, house or business. Insurance guarantees reimbursement for your belonging should something happen to it. You pay in premiums after the insurer evaluates the risk and the value of your belonging. You can buy health insurance, car insurance, home insurance, and more. The good thing about insurance is that it offers you peace of mind. If you own something valuable and it is insured, you are guaranteed repayment. Depending on your risk, your premiums could be really high, and usually you have to pay commission.

7. Property or Real Estate

This is an investment or a purchase of a home or any other kind of property, such as a business property. As an owner, this is a very lucrative and safe long-term investment option. If you choose to lease or rent out your property, you, as an owner, will make money off it. This gives you stable and positive cash flow. If your property gets damaged due to fire or other natural disasters, you, as the owner, will be liable. The maintenance costs can also count against you. Your property's value for sale is pegged to the interest rate. A higher interest rate increases the value, making it more expensive. You can also look into putting your property on Airbnb. It's a short-term rental option. It's lucrative given that you get to decide how much you would charge. It may not be stable, and it might take a while before your earnings can take off, because sales are solely based on your reputation. The disadvantage is that there is a high maintenance fee—which includes utilities and furnishing.

Investments and Fees

There are so many different investment options out there and choosing the best one(s) for yourself will be challenging. Truth is, you won't know how good or bad a stock or bond is until you actually give it a shot.

Some investment facilities require a minimum deposit to open an account. The amount depends on the type of investment you are opening. We recommend having a minimum deposit of at least £700 to £1,000. Some facilities don't require a minimum deposit, others may lower the costs, such as trading fees and account management fees. You have to shop around to find an investment option that is affordable and suitable for you.

Another fee that you must look out for are brokerage fees. This is what you pay to a financial broker to help you through the process of investing. They charge you for offering their expert advice and intel on the market and they will charge you every time you decide to buy or sell a stock. If you do this frequently, then your broker's fee will increase, along with the profitability of your earnings. Trading fees can amount to anything between £2 and £10 per trade for some discount brokers (Langager, 2019).

Don't let these additional charges put you off, though. You're better off getting help to create a solid investment portfolio than to create a clumsy one that incurs losses all the time, especially when you're starting out. You can otherwise approach a broker who charges no fees directly.

Full-service brokers give you the entire package. They provide financial advice for retirement, healthcare, life insurance and various other services. Full-service brokers are not cheap. In addition to charging you for advice, they also take a cut of your transactions and from the assets that they manage. Some even charge an annual membership fee.

Thanks to technology, there are digital platforms that do the investing for you. We told you about robo-advisors earlier in this chapter. They are automated, algorithm-driven, financial planning tools that not only help you plan your finances, but also create portfolios for you. They are usually free of charge. It's heaven if you're an introvert.

As you start off, it would be advisable to work with a broker or financial advisor, especially if you're going for those big accounts. Or you can continue to research and learn your way around it. Start small, make mistakes, learn from it, and you will get closer and closer to reaching your financial goals.

To recap, here's what you can do to increase your wealth:

1. Set aside 10% of earnings to pay yourself to accumulate wealth.
2. Save your money in a tax-free account like an Individual Savings Account (ISA) that is well-priced with fair benefits.
3. Spread your risk by diversifying your saving and investing across portfolios and countries: Geographically diversified (70%), commodities (20%), and keeping (some) cash in reserve (10%).

If you want to grow your money faster with the least bit of effort, explore passive income accounts or increase your exposure across a number of different funds to make more money simultaneously.

As with anything in life, there are some (golden) rules to bear in mind when you invest:

1. The greater return you want, the more risk will be involved.
2. Try to diversify as much as you can to lower your risk exposure, i.e., invest in different companies, industries, and regions.

3. You can achieve better outcomes if you save for a longer period of time. Try to invest for at least five years; alternatively, use a short-term investment account like cash savings.

4. Once you start investing, stay informed on how each of your accounts are performing. You will have to review your accounts regularly to notice if there are gaps you can fill to complete your portfolio, or to remove accounts that are resulting in losses instead of gains.

5. Don't panic. Investments can change their trajectory at any point. Decide if it is in your best interest to buy or sell.

Chapter 5:

How to Manage Your

Growing Wealth

Now that you've got your wealth building in different accounts, you can sit back and relax. Your money is safe and growing and you don't have to chase after it any longer. What you do have to do, though, is maintain the growth.

The accounts you have invested in each have their own regulations and policies to help your money grow, but it is still your money, so you still need to keep a record of how it is growing. At the same time, you need to keep finding ways that you can accelerate the growth in these accounts.

Remember the 'pay yourself first' rule? That applies throughout your wealth creation journey. You have to get into the habit of saving more than you spend, especially if your goal is to create more wealth.

We know it's tempting to want to splurge as soon as your bank balance recovers, which is okay. You're allowed to spoil yourself once in a while but remember that saving your money is also something you're doing *for* yourself. For *your* future self. The impulse you should have upon seeing your new bank balance is to *want* to save money. As was advised in the previous chapter, save at least 10% of your income. Pay off your debts and expenses second, and if you have any more money remaining, you can splurge on the shoes you've been eyeing for a while.

An easy way to remember to pay yourself when you get your income is to set a reminder on the same day of each month. It can either be at the start or at the end of the month, just ensure that you are saving consistently. You don't have to invest it immediately. For the time being, you can hold it in your savings account or money market account—until you decide which account to put it in.

Something called Direct Debit can also help you with the savings process.

Direct Debit is a payment system that uses your permission to make automated transactions between accounts, such as your own account and that of a business or organization. You will be notified of the dates and amounts to be collected (in case you forget).

Once you have set up the system, money will be deducted on a monthly basis or however often you need to make payments. The money deducted will usually be a standard amount unless you or the other part decides to change it. Either party would have to be notified of the change. The automated payments take the pressure off you to pay each account separately, which can result in mistakes, but it also gives you a clear indication of how much money you need exactly to cover your expenses and to save.

When you pay for things manually, it's hard to keep track of how much money you started with and how much money is leaving your account. If your payments are not properly organised it may be difficult for you to identify if money has mysteriously left your account.

The introduction of a system like Direct Debit brings some structure and organization to your finances. It removes stress and gives you peace of mind, because let's be honest, nobody likes to think of bills. The plus side, you'll get a pleasant surprise when you open your savings account, especially if you haven't been actively watching your money move into your savings. Seeing a healthy bank balance only further encourages you to save more money. Then there's the reward of having the money there when you need it, instead of scrambling and waiting for your next paycheck. You can never lose when you save more.

Time Is Money

There's a reason the stock market is referred to as 'gambling.' Both require you to put money in to get more out. Sometimes you win and sometimes you lose more than you put in. It's a calculated risk and that's just the rule of the game.

The stock market moves by the second, they are volatile, unpredictable and there are no guarantees of solid returns. Investors and financial advisors keep a close eye on market trade to identify the most lucrative investment choice at that moment, but what might look good at 12:00 P.M. in the afternoon can lose all its value at close. You never know when you're going to win and when you're going to lose.

There's an ongoing debate between investors to determine what is the best strategy to successful investing.

On one side there is 'market timing' and the other side is 'the time in the market.'

Let's break it down.

'Market timing' is when an investor or stockbroker tries to predict *when* a good time is to buy and sell their stock. The idea is to buy low and sell high, but there's no knowing when is the ideal time to make a transaction due to the volatile nature of the market. The only thing they can really rely on is the performance of the stock on that particular day or its overall performance over a period of time. Although, this can change in an instant, so trying to predict what might happen to the share price of a stock throughout the day is an almost futile task. The rewards are short-term. You can take an educated guess, but that too may not always lead you to the treasure. This strategy therefore doesn't have a 100% success rate when it comes to growing your wealth. You may be struck by luck every once in a while, but that's also just another rule of the game. Additionally, if you have a broker, you may have to cough up extra money to pay them for buying and selling stocks on the market for you. This fee will also increase as you choose to buy and sell more—you have to pay the commission even if you didn't make a profit. Given the unpredictable nature of the market, it would be safer and wiser to not depend on the timing of the market to trade your stocks.

'Time in the market' refers to the duration that you have kept your investments in the market. This is the better option if you're trying to build your wealth. The longer you leave your finances in the market, the faster it will grow, that's thanks to the magic of compounding. Leaving your stocks in the market regardless of changes requires patience, but the returns are more guaranteed then when you would depend on market timing to make your money. Your earnings will be steady, and you have a higher guarantee, plus, you don't have to do anything, because it is a passive form of income. Another advantage is that you, as the investor, will ride out the natural cycle of the market. Your earnings could fluctuate, but at least, they'll be there. This is an especially helpful method of saving if you're looking to make a big purchase like a car or house.

Asset Classes

Financial products or securities that share similar characteristics such as regulations, laws, and policies are classified into an asset class. They intend to help investors diversify their portfolios, spread risk, and earn differing returns. Asset classes are grouped by virtue of their cash flow stream and risks. Diversifying your investment portfolio helps you build more wealth at a faster pace.

When investing in different types of asset classes, it's important to note what can influence changes and rates of return

There are four types of asset classes. These include:

- Equities (stocks) are shares owned by publicly owned companies. Shares will most likely be influenced by investors' perceptions of the financial standing of the company that owns them. If a company is performing poorly, investors are likely to sell those stocks. This affects the share price and the dividends that a shareholder will receive. Stocks provide high returns, but it's accompanied by risks.

- Fixed income (bonds) are issued by governments or companies to help them raise money to fund projects, or in the case of businesses, to expand projects. Investors earn a fixed annual interest on bonds and are repaid the principal amount of the bond once it reaches maturity. Bonds are pretty stable; however, the interest rate can affect them. When interest rates increase, the value of your bond will decrease, making it harder to sell because it has less value compared to bonds issued with the new interest rate. Low interest rates increase the value of the bond you hold.

- Cash equivalents is the cash stored in a savings account as a short-term investment. Cash equivalents are highly liquid and have a high credit profile. They are low-risk with low-return profiles. Cash equivalents include Treasury bills, bank certificates of deposit, bankers' acceptances, corporate commercial paper, and other money market instruments. Cash equivalents in businesses also act as capital or net worth, to pay off debt, expenses, and to buy inventories. Cash equivalents are influenced by foreign exchange reserves and the exchange rate, as explained in Chapter 1.

- Property investments generate income by leasing the property out to renters, who would pay a monthly fee to the owner or landlord. The real estate market is said to be the most stable and lucrative form of investment. Interest rates can affect the price of buying property, but the actual value of housing can only significantly be impacted by the economy as a whole, as we saw with the 2008 global financial crisis.

How to Keep Track of Your Portfolio

We mentioned that saving money in investment accounts count as passive income, because wealth accumulates by itself, but since it is your money and your earnings, it is crucial for you to keep track of how much you are earning and at what rate.

If you have invested in equities, especially, it would be important for you to keep an eye on how the business itself is performing. You can keep track of the New York Stock Exchange, under equities. If the business is performing poorly, then it would be advisable to try to sell your stock at a high price and invest in another, better performing stock. But also bear in mind the difference between market timing and time in a market. Only sell your stock if you are at risk of huge losses but try as best as you can to save your money over long periods of time to ensure a steadier return.

Where bonds and real estate are concerned, it will be important for you to keep an eye on interest rates. A high interest rate is likely to decrease the value of your bond. If money is owed to you, a high interest rate will benefit you, but if you are owing money, it will increase the amount that you owe. In the property market, a decrease in interest rates will make buying a house for a cheaper price but a lower interest rate also means you earn less on your savings and investments. Like we said, there's a lot to gain and lose in the world of money.

As you build your knowledge and understand the inner workings of every financial product and how the changes influence you, you begin to make better choices with your money. Learning empowers you, boosts your confidence, and strengthens your financial independence, as American businessman Robert Kiyosaki once said:

"The truth is that money doesn't make you rich, knowledge does."

Chapter 6:

Overcoming Financial

Inhibitions

How many times have you looked at a clothing item or appliance in a store and thought, "If only I could afford this!"

Money either controls us or we control it. The way you define your relationship with money will determine the power dynamic between you and your money.

If you're struggling to make ends meet because you don't have enough money, you are likely to have negative feelings toward it. It forces you to wake up early in the morning, drive through traffic, and sit at a desk for eight hours every day to earn your bread. It feels like we do a lot just to earn money.

We sacrifice a lot for money too. So much of our time goes towards making a living that we forget to live a life. We're so caught up in the chase that our hobbies, our families, and even our own wellbeing takes a back seat. When you start ignoring your health and family to make money, it becomes easy to hate the mere existence of money, because the more you need it, the more it controls you, robbing you of your freedom and space.

We need money to survive, that IS the truth. We need it to cover our basic needs like food, water, shelter, education, clothing, and more, but we don't JUST need them to survive; being able to afford food, water, shelter, and education also just improves the way you live.

If you look at money as a means to live, instead of life itself, you will begin to see how you control it and not the other way around.

Money makes things possible. Think about how you were able to afford your child's education, how you were able to afford a family holiday, or how your hard-earned money gave you the home you're living in now.

Money made it possible, and it was you who enabled that possibility.

When you recognise what money has done for you, you appreciate it more. You also appreciate the things that money gave you, like your home or that once-in-a-lifetime experience.

The first step of financial freedom is to change your mindset. You may have heard at least one of the following quotes in your lifetime:

"Money is the root of all evil."

"Money brings you happiness."

"Money makes the world go round."

Common phrases like these are bound to shape your perception of money, thus changing the way you relate to it. A few bad experiences with money will even have you believing that money is the root of all evil. Or that you can only be happy if you have enough money, but here's the thing: Money itself does not cause evil and money itself does not bring happiness, but the way you use money does.

As we explained at the beginning of this book: Money can exist, but it's the value that we as humans put on it that makes it important.

If we look at money differently, we use it differently. One way to change your perception of money is to look at how much money you do have, not how much money you don't have.

Read that again.

Look at how much money you do have, not how much money you don't have.

Then, you can think about how you can use it better.

That's the foundation of wealth creation. It's about taking what you have and getting the best use out of it.

Think about what we spoke about in Chapter 3 on wealth. Wealth can only be created when you have something to build on. You could have £100, but with the proper strategies, choices, and knowledge, you can get the best use out of that £100. The best way you can get the most out of a £100 is to invest it. Invest it in all the ways we have been talking about until now.

Your wealth has the potential to grow as much and for as long as you want it to. You control money, money does not control you. The sooner you realise this, the better.

The children's book called *The Goose that Laid the Golden Egg* provides a good lesson on how money and wealth has the power to control you, if you let it (Patterson & Aesop, 1988). It goes something like this.

There once lived a farmer and his wife. They were not exceptionally rich, but with the little they had, they were happy. The farmer would harvest fruit and vegetables from his farm and sell it at the market. The farmer earned a simple and honest living. They didn't have a lot, but at the time, they had enough. The farmer had some chickens and a goose that would lay eggs that he'd sell as well. Still, the money wasn't a lot. The goose had not laid any eggs, until one day, when it laid a golden egg. The farmer knew that the golden egg would be worth so much more than the regular, white eggs that the chickens laid. He began to sell the golden eggs at a really high price. The goose laid a golden egg every day and the farmer sold it in return for big amounts of money. The farmer and his wife were now rich; they owned a big luxurious house. Now that they had too much money, they wanted more and more. The farmer and his wife had become pretty greedy. They wondered what would happen if they could sell all the golden eggs at once, instead of waiting for an egg every day. The farmer and his wife decided that they would cut the goose open and get all of its eggs at once. Greed had gripped the couple and they didn't care about the goose. They only cared about the golden eggs it could give. They cut the goose open to get the eggs, but to their dismay, there were no eggs and they had killed the goose. The farmer and his wife lost all their riches to greed.

The Goose that Laid the Golden Egg provides a good lesson on how money, when used incorrectly, can lead you down a dark road. Basically, money is not evil; it's the people who make it evil. It's the people who use it in the wrong way that make us think that money itself is bad or is the root of all evil. A corrupt politician was always corrupt, money just made it visible.

In the same way, money itself does not bring you happiness, but the way you use it can. Money is also used for noble reasons, for example, to raise money for good causes, to give to charities, and to give to the underprivileged. The act of giving money, for a good cause, instead gives you happiness.

This quote by Jim Carey, actor, and comedian, sums up the relationship between money and happiness perfectly:

"I think everybody should get rich and famous and do everything they ever dreamt of so they can see that it's not the answer."

In this way, you can think about what money does for you and not what you do for money. Working is one part of your life, but not your entire life. Similarly, money is part of your life, not your life itself.

What Is Your Relationship With Money?

Here are three things you can do to improve your relationship with money.

1. Identify what matters to you and then think about how you have been able to obtain it and how you will obtain it in the future. It doesn't have to be material, it can be that holiday you were able to take, or the priceless smile on your mother's face when you bought her a beautiful gift for her birthday. Recognize that although money made those things possible, it did not define it. Sometimes just spending time with your mother will make her smile.

2. It's what you have that matters. Wealth builds on money you already have. As we explained

above, when you concentrate on what you have instead of what you want, you begin to see the potential to create, rather than worrying that you could lose money and failing to start saving anyway.

3. Money does not define you. The money that you have stored as wealth, or in the form of your Michael Kors bag or diamond ring is not who you are, it's just what you have. Your money is not who you are, it is only what you have. Don't compete with others either. Everyone has different reasons for wanting to create wealth, yours may not be as elaborate as your friend's, and that's okay. It's your money and you get to decide what to do with it and what role it plays in your life.

Answer either 'yes,' 'no,' or 'sometimes' to the questions below to help you discover your relationship with money (Champion, n.d.).

1. I dread sitting down and paying my bills.
2. I spend more as I make more money.
3. I exaggerate the amount of money I have.
4. I am tense and my stomach is in knots when I think about my finances.
5. I am envious of the amount of money others have.
6. I get confused when making money decisions.

7. I think that getting a large sum of money will solve all my money problems, like winning the lottery or a large inheritance.

8. I get concerned when the stock market goes down.

9. I have a habit of waiting until the last minute to pay bills. It could be waiting til I get reminder calls, filing an extension on my income taxes, or running down to the utilities company before I get a late fee.

10. I feel sorry for those who have less money.

11. I have regrets over my past financial decisions, thinking I could have spent my money wiser.

12. I worry about my future ability to make ends meet.

13. I don't take time to appreciate what I have, always wanting more.

14. I try to get attention using my money, whether it's picking up the tab, or bragging about my new car.

15. I spend money when I need a pick-me-up. (Champion, n.d.)

If you answered 'yes' to most questions, then you need to reevaluate your relationship with money. Money will always exist, and we will always need it, but remember to focus on what you have over what you don't; and if you think about money as a problem, rather remember all the things that money made possible for you.

Chapter 7:

Positive vs Negative

Energy Toward Money

The Law of Attraction states that positive thoughts invite positive changes into one's life, while negative thoughts invite negative changes into a person's life. According to the Law of Attraction, everything exists as energy. When you have a positive mindset, you invite more positive changes into your life. This can impact your health, finances, and relationships.

If everything is energy, then so is money. Energy is present in the transactions you make; in the money you earn and the money you give. The energy comes from you, and it's based on what you're thinking when you're giving and receiving money.

Think about it, how would you feel if a friend asked you to lend them some money? Would you feel comfortable knowing you're helping a friend in need, or would you feel uncomfortable because you're not sure if your friend will pay it back?

Both these responses are energetic manifestations in your body. They're a reaction to your thoughts, and it tells you how you feel about money. Interesting right?

Option A: You say yes to your friend because you trust them, and you understand your 'yes' energy brings in more positivity. What you give is what you get.

Option B: You say no to your friend because you don't trust them, and you feel that you will lose money if you give it to them. By saying no, you may close the channel to receive more money.

As we highlighted in Chapter 6 on Overcoming Financial Inhibitions, you have to change your mindset to change your relationship with money. Having a positive relationship with money will give you the freedom to channel it in the right way, to things that matter to you. As soon as you recognize that money works for you, and not the other way around, you become more appreciative of the currency.

Appreciation and gratitude is another language that the universe understands. The Law of Attraction states that more comes to those who are thankful for what they have. Practising gratitude is an easy way to raise your vibration and change your energy towards money. Those who are ungrateful have more to lose than gain, while those who are grateful send a message to the universe saying, "thank you for what I have." The universe responds by giving more.

Gratitude is the practice of focusing on what you have instead of what you don't have, as illustrated in Chapter 6. You will attract more of what you want because you opened a channel of receiving.

The world of money operates in a similar way. If you give more, you're likely to receive more. For example, if you invest more money into an account, you will get more money in return. Does it make sense?

If the Law of Attraction is something that doesn't quite make sense to you, then that's okay. Don't fret, though, it doesn't mean you won't make your money.

The point, however, is understanding that there IS an energy transfer when we make transactions. You may not be aware of it, but it does exist. The energy influences money-making decisions, it influences how and what you buy, how and what you sell, and what you choose to keep.

Money is power and that power is energy.

Here's a snippet on what it means to align with the energy of money and abundance (Your Youniverse, 2017).

"If your goal is to manifest money so you may feel free or secure in the future, the vibration of your present moment is what will need to change. You will need to match that energetic component in the now, versus hoping money will manifest for you later down the line or in the future. If you believe that in the present moment you lack freedom and security, and you are asking for abundance to show up and correct this for you, you will be in a present state of 'lack' which is not a match to what you want. Additionally, it's the freedom and security you're actually seeking, not the middleman of money. Money is simply a means to obtain that freedom and security. To manifest the things we want, we must each develop a healthy energetic relationship with those things. When we don't work on this, we are only using part of our manifestation power."

"Abundance is everywhere. It's our perception and energetic relationship with money that may make it seem otherwise. For most of us, we are never more than a few feet away from a lot of money. Millions of pounds in fact. Think about the amount of money that is at your local bank or even multiple local banks, or in the safes in the businesses near you. This money is also constantly being exchanged energetically throughout the internet every moment of every day. In truth, money is constantly surrounding you. It's always present and nearby. Even if you don't see it, it's there. What this means is, in actuality, you are only a few feet away from the freedom, security and luxury that you truly want."

You first need to be aware of the actual energy before harnessing it to invite positive changes in your life. In order to do this, you need to do more good. Light attracts light in the law of attraction.

Here's what you can do:

1. Donate to Charity

You have money, so why not share it? There are people in the world who do not own even half of what you have. There are people struggling for food, water, shelter, and other basic needs. They need people like you and me to make their lives easier. There's a difference between being a wealthy person and a hoarder. A wealthy person not only knows how to make money, but also how and when to give money. Let your other wealth be your kindness. So, every once in a while, buy a trolley full of food and deliver it to a charity organisation, an old-age home, or to other people in need. Giving is an act of love; the universe understands the energy of love. The more love you give, the more love you get. As you're doing this, be aware of how you feel. How do you feel when a little child smiles at you for giving them a hot plate of food? How do you feel when an old woman tells you "Thank you, you made my day"? How do you feel when a disabled person tells you you made them feel seen? If you're feeling happy, emotional, and loving, then that's a feeling you need to hold on to and harness in your everyday life. The more you focus on those positive energies every day, the more likely you will receive.

2. Be Grateful for What You Have

The universe responds to feelings of gratitude and appreciation. It does not respond to feelings of resentment and jealousy. When you earn money on your investments, be grateful for it. It may not be as much as you wanted it to be, but it's something that you received. It also applies to when you receive your work salary, a bonus or even just a gift. Don't complain. It will lower your vibration. Just like how you're seeking to build your wealth—you need to raise your vibrations to receive more and be more accepting of what you're receiving in the present moment. If you stop it, you won't know what blessings you're missing out on.

3. Do More of What Makes You Happy

Do you enjoy dancing? Then dance. Do you enjoy painting? Then paint. Do you enjoy gardening? Then don't let anyone stop you. Choosing to do what makes you happy is a love language in itself. It's you, giving yourself love. If you feel more love, happiness, and peace within yourself, the more likely you are to share it with others. Your positive energy changes your thoughts and the way you see the world. The world looks like a better place when you're in a better space. The possibilities seem endless, and you will have the confidence to claim it all. Remember, don't keep your happiness to yourself, the world can always use more people who seek solutions and who want to make the world a better place.

4. Cultivate Good Habits

Eating healthy, exercising frequently, practicing meditation, getting enough sleep, and surrounding yourself with good people are ways for you to become a better person. When your body is healthy, your mind becomes healthy. Let go of any harmful habits such as smoking or excessive use of alcohol and meditate more often. Meditation helps you become more self-aware, and when you're more aware, you pay more attention to your choices, especially financially. We know that emotions tend to run high in the stock market, so maintaining calm in high-stress situations can help you make more sound and decisions. Start with making small positive changes daily until they become your lifestyle. This is another way you can take more control and manage your life better.

5. Forgive and Let Go

If a past relationship or job is still holding you down, take active steps in forgiving yourself and then the other person. Through meditation and awareness, you can learn to be honest with yourself and accept reality for what it is. Holding onto the past only stops us from moving forward into becoming happier and healthier. Pain is part of any process in life and while it might be difficult to see past it, be grateful for the lessons it's given you and how those lessons are going to carry you through the next stage of your life, whether it's a relationship, a job or even a completely new lifestyle.

Working With Affirmations

Working with affirmations helps you stay positive in mind and in action. Affirmations are basically positive statements or mantras that you say out loud or to yourself to replace negative thoughts with positive ones. When you repeat the statements, you begin to believe them. Think of it as a mental exercise to improve your mental health and mental strength. Here is a list of money affirmations for you to work with (Avila, 2019).

I am a money magnet.

Money flows freely to me.

I release all resistance to attracting money. I am worthy of a positive cashflow.

There is always more than enough money in my life.

I naturally attract good fortune.

I am financially free.

My income exceeds my expenses.

I deserve to be paid for my skills, time, and knowledge.

I have a positive relationship to money and know how to spend it wisely.

My income increases constantly.

I am wealthy in more ways than one.

My job/business allows me to live the life I desire.

I am connected to the universal supply of money.

I am grateful for the abundance that I have and the abundance on its way.

Every pound I spend and donate comes back to me multiplied.

I can look at my finances without fear.

I choose to live a rich and full life.

I give myself permission to prosper and grow.

I am worthy of all the richness I desire.

I have the power to create the success and build the wealth I desire (Avila, 2019).

Repeat these affirmations as many times as you like. When you release good intentions for yourself, the universe responds to it and delivers it to you. What you give is what you will receive. We all coexist on this beautiful planet, so there is no harm in offering a helping hand to one in need sometimes. Use your privilege to help others, and you WILL reap the rewards for your actions.

Chapter 8:

The Path to Freedom

"How do you eat an elephant? One bite at a time."

That's the common phrase used to describe how we can take on life's big and daunting tasks: You take one step at a time.

The world of finance is not exactly easy to navigate. Think of it as a huge and elaborate maze. At the centre of the maze is wealth and everyone on this maze can get a share of it. There are several routes that you can take to get to the centre, some of them are narrow and risky, others are broad and often you're not alone on this path. Everyone discovers a different route to get to the centre, with time they even become familiar with the different routes. Some people take longer to get there, some people hit one or several dead ends, some people work together to get there faster. Whichever direction is taken, everyone is ultimately on the same route. It all started with one step! One step to enter the maze and several steps to move forward.

You, dear reader, have taken that first step! So, congratulations for that. You are now on your way towards a better financial future. With the knowledge you have gained up until now, the path ahead may be less daunting.

You will encounter several challenges, though. You may hit dead ends and even lose money along the way. But as we said before, that's just how the game of investing works. You have to lose some to gain some, and whatever obstacle you face on this journey, there is one thing you should remember: Why you started in the first place.

Start by reminding yourself of your dreams.

What sort of life did you envision for yourself and for your family? Did you compile a bucket list at university, but failed to go through with it because life happened? Why not pick it up again and see if you'd still like to do some of the things—maybe shark cave diving or taking a trip with your best friends to a foreign land. Your values may have changed since then, so better yet why not create a bucket list with new ideas and experiences you would like to have. Maybe travel is still on that list. Alongside climbing Mount Everest, perhaps you would like to start your own business, and now seems like the perfect time.

Think about your goals and dreams, even if they seem unattainable or out of reach. Write them down and keep them close so you can see them every day. It will serve as a reminder of why you should take another step on your financial journey. Seeing a list of your dreams on paper makes them seem more attainable. It encourages you and gives you a sense of direction.

Psychology says setting goals helps us create a more meaningful, satisfying, and successful life. There are different methods to help you achieve those goals; you have to decide what works for you. Perhaps you need to take a course to fulfill your dream of becoming an animator or graphic designer, or you need to start music classes to achieve your lifelong dream of becoming a guitarist. Your dreams are possible; your actions set them in motion.

Courtesy of *The Only Way to Eat an Elephant*, here is a five-step plan that you can follow to attain your goals (Frankenfield, 2019).

Frankenfield, who writes for Psychology Today, describes it as the SMART guide. SMART stands for: Specific, Measurable, Attainable, Relevant, and Time-bound.

Let's explore what they each mean and how you can best execute it.

1. Be Specific

Setting a goal means that you have an idea of what you want but adding details to the idea is what will make execution easier. So, if you're thinking of creating wealth, put a number and a date to it. For example, "I would like to earn £20,000 a month by the time I am 30," or "I need to make £15,000 in the next five months so I can take my family on holiday." When you set specific targets for yourself instead of just goals, you can keep track of how far you've come on your savings journey and how far you are yet to go. It also helps to visualize your end goal. Perhaps you can visualize a cheque with the figure £15,000 on it, or you can keep a picture of that holiday destination you would like to go to close by.

2. Measure Your Progress

Again, don't think of your goal as one huge idea that's just going to happen. You have to make it happen and even if you feel your goal is 'too big' or 'too farfetched.' The truth is that if you can dream it, you can do it. So, break down the big goal into smaller, more manageable pieces that you can work with day-by-day or week-by-week. Maybe keep a list of what you hope to achieve in that week and cross it off once complete. If you're planning that trip, for example, start looking for accommodation, check if your passport is up to date, look for fair plane tickets. It's not just measuring, it's also just good planning. There's something satisfying about getting stuff done.

3. Make It Attainable

Unless, by some miracle you earn a windfall gain, it's not going to be possible to make £100,000 in one week. If only things were THAT easy, right? You have to be practical in order for your goals to materialise. Don't set really high expectations that the mere thought of doing it turns you off. You don't want to achieve the 'impossible,' you rather want to go for what's attainable. If you find that your goals kind of exceed your resources like time, money, and capacity, you might want to make some adjustments that will still let you meet a goal that's closest and more practical. In this scenario, aim to make your £100,000, but at least give yourself a year or more. You can get what you want, sometimes it just takes a little bit longer.

4. Is It Relevant?

Think about the goals you're setting and ask yourself, why? Why is it so important for you to turn this goal into a reality? How will it change your life and how will it change or influence the lives around you? Does it align with who you are and finally how does it actually make you feel? If you choose a goal that makes you want to spring into action every time you think about it, then you're on the right track, but if thinking about it in the long run drains you and seems boring, then maybe let go and find something that really sets your heart on fire. It's normal to feel scared when you're about to take a huge step, not knowing what's on the other side; don't let it stop you, though. If it's something your heart is really set on, then be willing to take some (practical) risks to achieve it.

5. Manage Your Time

Manage your time and your expectations. If you know something NEEDS to get done by a certain date or even time, plan ahead. Find a method that helps you use your time more efficiently. If, for example, you know that you're more productive in the mornings, then try to get most of your work done then. If the task seems too big to achieve in a day, break it into little chunks and assign deadlines to each of those. It will keep the momentum going. We all have the same 24 hours in a day; it's how you use it that matters.

When your goal is clear and the road to achieving it seems doable, then it's all up to you to set things into motion. Your desires should propel you and your plan should get you there faster.

Values vs Goals

When you're feeling uninspired, you may want to take a step back, instead of forcing yourself into a situation that may not reap favourable results. It's okay to pause, but don't stop. If you still need to measure your goal setting personality, answer the questions below either with 'often' 'sometimes' or 'rarely.' Using the SMART plan, see how you can improve your objectives or align your goals with your values (*How Good Is Your Goal Setting? Are You Meeting Your Goals, or Missing Out?* 2009).

1. I set lots of goals in the hope that I will achieve some of them.
2. I find that my targets are too ambitious.

3. If I'm struggling to meet a goal, I set sub-goals to renew my motivation.
4. I don't celebrate success until I've achieved a goal.
5. I tie my work-related objectives to my personal ambitions.
6. I set low standards so that my goals are easy to meet.
7. I don't ask for support from friends and colleagues if I become demotivated.
8. I celebrate my success when I hit my targets.
9. I think about what my boss or family wants me to achieve when I set personal goals.
10. I regularly monitor how I am doing, so that I can measure how well I am progressing towards my goals.
11. My personal values aren't relevant to my work-related objectives.
12. I don't set an end date for achieving my goals, so that I give myself plenty of time.
13. I seek out tools that help me reach my goals.
14. When I make new plans, I reflect on my existing commitments to make sure that I don't take on too much.
15. If I fail to meet a target, I move on without reflecting on what went wrong.
16. I look for ways to build goals into my daily life by developing new habits.
17. I get excited by new ideas, and I flit from goal to goal without achieving anything.

18. I enjoy planning how to achieve goals, but then get bored by the mundane work of delivering them.

After you identify your goals and values, organise it into needs and wants so that your priorities are clearer to you. This will help you move along your path even faster.

Conclusion:

Money. But Not as We Know It

What is your relationship with money?

Is it something that you have power over or something that has power over you?

As we explored in *Focused Financial Literacy, The Starting Point for Financial Success,* you are the only one who has control over your money. Money is only as important as the value that you put on it. Without value, money is merely a piece of paper, a coin, or a number.

The Spanish conquistadors who sought to acquire all the gold and riches from the New World taught us that even though they were rich in gold, the gold had no real value. The Spaniards did not know how to use the gold, so instead of becoming rich, the Spanish economy collapsed.

Currency is different from money. Currency is the physical article used to make an exchange, and this can vary from coins to grain and weapons, as early hunter gatherers demonstrated through the method of bartering. No standard value system existed; it was the parties involved who instead decided how an item should be valued.

Centuries later, this didn't change. The money we use today wouldn't exist if it wasn't for the value we put on it, what we decide to use it for.

Money has many different uses. The most common is to pay for things. It makes things possible, but it is not everything. Money can also be used to create wealth.

Wealth is what remains after our debts and expenses have been paid off. Another word for wealth is net worth. In companies, net asset value is what's left after its liabilities are subtracted from its total assets. It's measured as either book value or shareholder's equity. This is essentially the returns received by the owner or shareholder of a company. A country's wealth is measured by its GDP. This is the total market value of the services and goods produced in the country during a period, usually annually. As we explained in Chapter 3 on wealth, when a country's GDP is high, the standard of living increases because the country has more money to provide better services and resources to its people. This can be in the form of better healthcare services, transport, high quality raw materials for food and clothing, etc.

Creating wealth is what gives you financial freedom, but before you take that step, you must understand how the financial system works. The financial system can be compared to a car. It has different components, each of which has a certain function, but which cannot function on its own; as we remind you, you are the fuel that keeps this system running.

That's because you're the one providing the money to make it move. You do that by saving and investing your money. If you have the desire to create wealth, instead of living from income to income, then you will realise that you have a very important role in the larger scheme of things.

It is through your saving and investing that banks create money to raise capital to loan to others. It works on the system of interest. Interest is earned on investments and loans. If you're a saver, interest is your best friend, but if you're a borrower, interest can cost you a lot more money. That's why it's important for you to be mindful and wise about where you put your money.

There are five key institutions that form the base for the financial products you can use to create wealth.

Briefly, these are credit and debit, bonds, joint-stock companies, insurance, and the property market.

Credit and debit is a book-keeping system used by companies to keep track of money that is going in and money that is going out. Debit is when money enters an account and credit is when money leaves an account.

The system was developed in ancient Babylon. A system was created to keep track of how much money was owed. They used clay tablets to keep track. The tablets were washed out once the debt was cleared. In some cases, if a borrower could not repay debts, which was usually made in the form of food, their debt-tablets were washed.

Trading money can easily go wrong, so one Italian mathematician named Luca Pacioli developed the 'double-entry bookkeeping system' to ensure the accurate flow of money. It was popularised by a powerful Italian family: de Medicis. The family used the system to create more wealth.

Bonds function as both a financial system as well as an investment facility. They are one of the most stable forms of an investment. Bonds are issued by governments or companies to raise capital. An investor will buy a bond at face value. For every year until it reaches maturity, the investor will earn interest. Once the bond reaches maturity, the principal amount is repaid to the investor.

A joint-stock company was created in the 17th Century by the Dutch. The main function of a joint stock is to accumulate money from shareholders to achieve certain outcomes. Each shareholder will own a portion of the company, giving them power to contribute to the company's decision-making.

The first form of an insurance company was invented in a coffee shop in the UK. Investing in insurance helps spread risk or cover losses of a prized possession like a car or house, in the event of an accident or natural disaster. The investor pays monthly premiums into their account. Depending on the account, the investor can earn interest, increasing the money stored in their account.

Finally, the property or real estate market is when you buy a property, either a house or a business office, to own or rent. The property market is a lucrative investment option because it is stable. If you're renting your property, you are guaranteed a monthly income. You can also look into the short-term rental property market such as Airbnb.

In addition to the above, you can also invest in stocks and equities. This is the direct trading of stocks between companies. The returns on stocks and equities is pretty high, but so is the risk. Plus, there's the additional costs and fees that you are required to pay to the financial broker, whose responsibility is to advise you on the market and help you buy and sell stocks. The payment model differs from broker to broker, but fees do apply.

To avoid this, you can choose to invest through digital trading platforms or index funds. Digital investing platforms have grown in popularity of late, increasing your investment options.

Cash investments are short-term stable investments. You can invest your money in either a savings account, a money market account, or a certificate of deposit (CD). Returns on each account differs.

A fund is a pool of capital that several investors have contributed to. Investors then use these funds to buy securities. Each investor retains control and ownership over their own shares. The different types of investment funds include mutual funds, exchange traded funds, money market funds and others.

Investing in commodities is also something you look into. This is to either invest in the actual commodity like gold, minerals, agriculture, or a stock that represents the commodity. The price is pegged to inflation which is an advantage. The higher the inflation rate, the greater the value of your commodity. Gold, oil, and base metals are three most commonly traded commodities. Investing in a commodity is one of the best ways to diversify your portfolio.

All these methods are a means of earning a passive income. Passive income or residual income is money earned through the growth in your investments. It supplements your active income and requires very little everyday effort. If you don't have an active income—something you earn from your 9–5 job and your passive income is the only money you're getting—then it would be advisable to keep close tabs on how much you are earning monthly and transfer it to your current account to cover your monthly or everyday expenses.

Keeping track of your investments and portfolios is as important as investing. If you invested in company stocks, for example, you would need to keep tabs on the actual performance of the company. This will give you an indication on when to buy and sell. Although, you must be wary of market timing. As we pointed out, being a successful investor is not about knowing when to invest, but about how long you have kept your investments for.

Before you dive into making your first investment, remember the three rules of creating wealth as told to by *The Richest Man in Babylon* by George S Clason.

1. Pay yourself first.
2. Keep your expenses low.
3. Invest what you save.

Your investing actions are determined by your mindset.

It's easy to let your emotions get the best of you while you invest, making you forget all the rules and tricks of the investment world.

It therefore is important for you to understand your relationship with money. We will all have different relationships with money, depending on what we were taught when we were younger or how we perceived the financial world—especially when we didn't understand it.

You may have heard the saying "money is the root of all evil" and believed it, especially seeing all kinds of white-collar crimes happening around the world, but as we pointed out: Money itself is not evil, it's the people who use money with evil intent that taints the quality of money. As we remind you, money has no value. It's you who gets to decide how important it is to you and how you wish to use it in the world.

If you have a negative attitude towards money, you will likely struggle to grow your wealth or take steps towards improving your financial position. In such cases, you must remind yourself what money has done for you: It's helped you buy a house, put your children through university, and also made it possible for you to experience your dream holiday. When you look at it this way, you will recognize that money can do more for you, than you do for it.

To better understand your relationship with money, you can also identify what matters to you and focus on what you already have.

As we pointed out in Chapter 6: It's what you have that matters. When you concentrate on what you have instead of what you want, you begin to see the potential to create, instead of what you could lose. When you have a positive attitude towards money, you will be open to the different possibilities of wealth creation. Fear will hold you back, but the right knowledge will give you the confidence to forge ahead.

Energy is present in all money and all transactions. Your energy changes when you give and receive money. If you are comfortable and positive about giving money, then you open channels to receiving money.

Energy works hand in hand with the Law of Attraction. The Law of Attraction states that positive thoughts invite positive changes into one's life, while negative thoughts invite negative changes into a person's life.

Basically, when you have a positive mindset, you invite positive changes into your life. This can impact your health, finances, and relationships.

In addition to positive energy, gratitude is another language that the universe understands. Gratitude is about being thankful for what you have instead of focusing on what you don't have. This also cultivates a positive energy within yourself. Remember, wanting what you have brings more of the same thing into your life.

Similarly, in finance if you give more, you're likely to receive more. For example, if you invest more money into an account, you will get more money in return.

If you're struggling to make sense of your relationship with money, you can first learn to repeat and internalise affirmations. Working with affirmations helps you stay positive about your desires.

We all have different reasons for wanting to make money. For you, it might be to save toward a comfortable retirement. For a friend, it might be to put their children through university or buy a new house. Whatever your needs may be, it's important that you keep your goals and values in mind. Remember the five steps to help you reach your goal:

1. Be specific
2. Measure your progress
3. Make it attainable
4. Is it relevant?
5. Manage your time

The journey towards reaching your financial goals is easier than you think. With the right knowledge, right mindset, and with goals that align with your values and needs, you can live the life you've always wanted.

So, go forth and conquer, dear reader. Everything you've ever wanted is on the other side of fear.

References

3 Medici banking innovations we still use today. (n.d.). Edology. https://www.edology.com/blog/accounting-finance/3-medici-banking-innovations/

8 Wealth Creation Tips That You Must Know | WiserAdvisor - Blog. (2019, August 18). Wiseadvisor.com. https://www.wiseradvisor.com/blog/financial-planning/wealth-creation-tips/.

Accounting Stuff. (2018). ACCOUNTING BASICS: Debits and Credits Explained. YouTube. https://www.youtube.com/watch?v=VhwZ9t2b3Zk

Amadeo, K. (2011). *Who Decides How Much Money Is Worth.* The Balance. https://www.thebalance.com/value-of-money-3306108

Amadeo, K. (2019). *How Treasury Bills, Notes and Bonds Work.* The Balance. https://www.thebalance.com/what-are-treasury-bills-notes-and-bonds-3305609

Amadeo, K. (2020, October 26). *Interest Rates and How They Work.* The Balance.

https://www.thebalance.com/what-are-interest-rates-and-how-do-they-work-3305855#:~:text=An%20interest%20rate%20is%20the,affect%20the%20cost%20of%20loans

Apprend. (2017, September 27). *The Joint Stock Company and Changing America- APUSH TV.* YouTube. https://www.youtube.com/watch?v=30ALWDns4og

Avila, T. (2019, August 19). *20 Money Mantras To Inspire Financial Freedom.* Girlboss. https://www.girlboss.com/read/money-mantras-affirmations

Bank's editorial team. (2020, May 11). *Tax Free Savings Account in the USA: Types and Benefits.* Banks.com. https://www.banks.com/articles/banking/savings-accounts/tax-free-savings-accounts/#:~:text=A%20tax%2Dfree%20savings%20accounts

Banton, C. (2021). *Underwriter Definition.* Investopedia. https://www.investopedia.com/terms/u/underwriter.asp#:~:text=Key%20Takeaways-

Barone, A. (2019). *Paper Money.* Investopedia. https://www.investopedia.com/terms/p/paper_money.asp

Barone, A. (2020). *No-Load Fund Definition.* Investopedia.

https://www.investopedia.com/terms/n/no-loadfund.asp

Baskerville, P. (2012, March 31). *The history and definition of "Debits and Credits" in accounting.* Basic Accounting Concepts. https://www.basicaccountingconcepts.education/the-history-and-definition-of-debits-and-credits-in-accounting/

bea.gov. (2021, January 28). *Gross Domestic Product, 4th Quarter and Year 2020 (Advance Estimate) | U.S. Bureau of Economic Analysis (BEA).* Www.bea.gov. https://www.bea.gov/news/2021/gross-domestic-product-4th-quarter-and-year-2020-advance-estimate#:~:text=Current%2Ddollar%20GDP%20decreased%202.3

Beattie, A. (2019). *The History Of Money: From Barter To Banknotes.* Investopedia. https://www.investopedia.com/articles/07/roots_of_money.asp

Bestinvest. (n.d.). *What is an ISA?* Bestinvest. https://www.bestinvest.co.uk/stocks-and-shares-isa/what-is-an-isa

Bondigas, A. (n.d.). *How to Keep Track of Passive Income.* Small Business - Chron.com. https://smallbusiness.chron.com/keep-track-passive-income-73931.html

Business Casual. (2018). When The Dutch Ruled The World: The Rise & Fall of the Dutch

East India Company. In. https://www.youtube.com/watch?v=ewCs5CF5HEg

Canstar. (2019, January 21). *What is compound interest?* YouTube. https://www.youtube.com/watch?v=lNK95khKvSk

Carey, T. W. (2020, October 29). *Best Robo-Advisors.* Investopedia. https://www.investopedia.com/best-robo-advisors-4693125

CFP, G. L., Ph D. (2019, November 22). *Council Post: What Is Your Relationship With Money?* Forbes. https://www.forbes.com/sites/forbesfinancecouncil/2019/11/22/what-is-your-relationship-with-money/?sh=630450d42ddb

Champion, V. (n.d.). *Money Quiz Do You Need to Change Your Relationship with Money?* https://vickiechampion.com/money-quiz/

Chappelow, J. (2020, November 21). *Expansionary Policy Definition.* Investopedia. https://www.investopedia.com/terms/e/expansionary_policy.asp#:~:text=Expansionary%20monetary%20policy%20works%20by

Chen, J. (n.d.-a). *Investment Fund.* Investopedia. https://www.investopedia.com/terms/i/investment-fund.asp#:~:text=An%20investment%20fund%20%20is%20a

Chen, J. (n.d.-b). *Tracker Fund*. Investopedia. Retrieved May 25, 2021, from https://www.investopedia.com/terms/t/tracke rfund.asp#:~:text=Tracker%20funds%20are%2 0also%20known

Chen, J. (2003, November 25). *Passive Income*. Investopedia. https://www.investopedia.com/terms/p/passiv eincome.asp

Chen, J. (2019a). *Alternative Investment Definition*. Investopedia. https://www.investopedia.com/terms/a/altern ative_investment.asp

Chen, J. (2019b). *Load Fund Definition*. Investopedia. https://www.investopedia.com/terms/l/loadfu nd.asp#:~:text=A%20load%20fund%20is%20a

Chen, J. (2020a). *Cash Investment*. Investopedia. https://www.investopedia.com/terms/c/cashin vestment.asp

Chen, J. (2020b, October 22). *Debt Instrument*. Investopedia. https://www.investopedia.com/terms/d/debti nstrument.asp

Chen, J. (2021, January 31). *Exchange Rate Definition*. Investopedia. https://www.investopedia.com/terms/e/excha ngerate.asp#:~:text=An%20exchange%20rate %20is%20the%20value%20of%20a%20country

Clason, G. S. (1926). *Richest Man In Babylon.* Penguin Books.

Clear, J. (n.d.). *Book Summary: The Richest Man in Babylon by George Clason.* James Clear. https://jamesclear.com/book-summaries/the-richest-man-in-babylon

Conquistador | Spanish history. (2019). In *Encyclopædia Britannica.* https://www.britannica.com/topic/conquistador-Spanish-history

Consumer Spending. (2019). Investopedia. https://www.investopedia.com/terms/c/consumer-spending.asp

Davenport, J. (2012, September 7). *Spanish Conquistadors and the looting of Mexican and Peruvian golden treasure.* Mining Weekly. https://www.miningweekly.com/article/spanish-conquistadors-and-the-looting-of-mexican-and-peruvian-golden-treasure-2012-09-07

De La Rosa, W. (2019). 3 psychological tricks to help you save money | The Way We Work, a TED series [YouTube Video]. YouTube. https://www.youtube.com/watch?v=DOisAG9yoNk

Defining Wealth | Understanding wealth is essential. (2018, August 30). W8 Advisory. https://w8advisory.com/our-insights/defining-wealth/#:~:text=Wealth%20gives%20us%20more%20options

Definitions and Types of Insurance. (n.d.). Saylordotorg.github.io. https://saylordotorg.github.io/text_law-for-entrepreneurs/s22-01-definitions-and-types-of-insur.html

Direct Debit. (n.d.). *What is Direct Debit.* Www.directdebit.co.uk. https://www.directdebit.co.uk/DirectDebitExplained/Pages/WhatIsDirectDebit.aspx

Downey, L. (2020, October 21). *Store Of Value Definition.* Investopedia. https://www.investopedia.com/terms/s/storeofvalue.asp

Economics Online. (2017). *The Housing Market | Economics Online.* Economicsonline.co.uk. https://www.economicsonline.co.uk/Competitive_markets/The_housing_market.html

Farrington, R. (2017, November 29). *How Honest Financial Advisors Should Disclose Their Fees.* The College Investor. https://thecollegeinvestor.com/20678/how-honest-financial-advisors-should-disclose-their-fees/

Farrington, R. (2020, March 10). *Best Free Investing Apps of 2021 | Free Stock Trading.* The College Investor. https://thecollegeinvestor.com/19598/investing-apps-invest-for-free/

Fernando, J. (2020, November 29). *Law of Supply and Demand.* Investopedia.

https://www.investopedia.com/terms/l/law-
of-supply-demand.asp

Fettke, K. (2020, December 10). *History of the
U.S. Housing Market: Great Depression to Donald
Trump.* RealWealth.
https://www.realwealthnetwork.com/learn/us-
housing-market-history/

Financial System. (2019). Investopedia.
https://www.investopedia.com/terms/f/financ
ial-system.asp

Fontinelle, A. (2019a). *Getting a Grip on Holding
Companies.* Investopedia.
https://www.investopedia.com/terms/h/holdi
ngcompany.asp

Fontinelle, A. (2019b). *How Good of an Investment
Is Life Insurance?* Investopedia.
https://www.investopedia.com/articles/active-
trading/120814/life-insurance-smart-
investment.asp

Fournier, D. (2018, April 24). *The Only Way to
Eat an Elephant | Psychology Today South Africa.*
Www.psychologytoday.com.
https://www.psychologytoday.com/za/blog/m
indfully-present-fully-alive/201804/the-only-
way-eat-
elephant#:~:text=Desmond%20Tutu%20once
%20wisely%20said

Frankenfield, J. (2019). *Robo-Advisor (Robo-
Adviser).* Investopedia.

https://www.investopedia.com/terms/r/roboadvisor-roboadviser.asp

FreshBooks. (n.d.). *What Is a Debit and Credit? Bookkeeping Basics Explained.* FreshBooks. https://www.freshbooks.com/hub/accounting/debit-and-credit

Ganti, A. (2019a). *Asset Class Definition.* Investopedia. https://www.investopedia.com/terms/a/assetclasses.asp

Ganti, A. (2019b). *Multiplier Effect.* Investopedia. https://www.investopedia.com/terms/m/multipliereffect.asp

Gov.UK. (2021, April 20). *UK enshrines new target in law to slash emissions by 78% by 2035.* GOV.UK. https://www.gov.uk/government/news/uk-enshrines-new-target-in-law-to-slash-emissions-by-78-by-2035#:~:text=change%20and%20energy-

Harrabin, R. (2021, April 20). Climate change: UK to speed up target to cut carbon emissions. *BBC News.* https://www.bbc.com/news/uk-politics-56807520

Hayes, A. (2019a). *Book Value.* Investopedia. https://www.investopedia.com/terms/b/bookvalue.asp

Hayes, A. (2019b). *Understanding Shareholder Equity – SE.* Investopedia.

https://www.investopedia.com/terms/s/share holdersequity.asp

Hayes, A. (2019c). *Understanding the Bond Market.* Investopedia. https://www.investopedia.com/terms/b/bond market.asp

History.com Editors. (2018, August 21). *Code of Hammurabi.* HISTORY. https://www.history.com/topics/ancient-history/hammurabi

How Good Is Your Goal Setting? Are You Meeting Your Goals, or Missing Out? (2009). Mindtools.com. https://www.mindtools.com/pages/article/goa l-setting-quiz.htm

Inman, R. (2019a, April 30). *Financial Literacy: How to Fail in America.* Financial Residency. https://financialresidency.com/financial-literacy-how-to-fail-in-america/

Inman, R. (2019b, October 21). *Your Relationship With Money Starts With These 7 Stages.* Financial Residency. https://financialresidency.com/relationship-with-money/

Investopedia. (2019). *Money.* Investopedia. https://www.investopedia.com/terms/m/mon ey.asp

Joseph, C. (2011). *The AIDA Process in Advertising.* Chron.com.

https://smallbusiness.chron.com/aida-process-advertising-10490.html

Kagan, J. (2019). *What Everyone Should Know About Insurance.* Investopedia. https://www.investopedia.com/terms/i/insurance.asp

Kapralos, C. (n.d.). *A Brief History of Loans | Lending in Ancient Mesopotamia, Greece, Middle Ages.* Www.koho.ca. https://www.koho.ca/learn/history-of-lending/

Kenton, W. (2019). *Barter (or Bartering) Definition.* Investopedia. https://www.investopedia.com/terms/b/barter.asp

Kenton, W. (2020, November 2). *Economy.* Investopedia. https://www.investopedia.com/terms/e/economy.asp

King, L. W. (2008). *The Avalon Project : Code of Hammurabi.* Avalon.law.yale.edu. https://avalon.law.yale.edu/ancient/hamframe.asp#:~:text=48.

Kiplinger's Personal Finance. (2017). Building a Foundation for Investing Success. www.wi65.com. https://www.wi65.com/wp-content/uploads/2017/08/IPT_Building-a-Foundation_National.pdf

Kurt, D. (2020). *How Currency Works*. Investopedia. https://www.investopedia.com/articles/investing/092413/how-currency-works.asp

Kusimba, C. (2017, June 20). *When – and why – did people first start using money?* The Conversation. https://theconversation.com/when-and-why-did-people-first-start-using-money-78887#:~:text=The%20Mesopotamian%20shekel%20%E2%80%93%20the%20first

Landinguin, D. (2019, December 17). *Introduction to the Financial System*. YouTube. https://www.youtube.com/watch?v=Sqq-XBZEH-4

Langager, C. (2019). *A Beginner's Guide to Stock Investing*. Investopedia. https://www.investopedia.com/articles/basics/06/invest1000.asp

Lehtonen, S. (2019, August 10). Investing in Stocks 101: The Beginning Investor's Guide To Making More Money. *Investor's Business Daily*. https://www.investors.com/how-to-invest/investors-corner/investing-in-stocks-101/

Lemke, T. (2020, August 4). *Pros and Cons of Airbnb as an Investment Strategy*. The Balance. https://www.thebalance.com/pros-and-cons-of-airbnb-as-an-investment-strategy-4776231

Liodus, N. (2020, August 8). *The Inverse Relationship Between Interest Rates and Bond Prices*.

Investopedia.
https://www.investopedia.com/ask/answers/w
hy-interest-rates-have-inverse-relationship-
bond-prices

Mark Richard Greene. (2018). Insurance -
Historical development of insurance. In
Encyclopædia *Britannica.*
https://www.britannica.com/topic/insurance/
Historical-development-of-insurance

Mbara, N. (2021, May 8). *Common money saving*
mistakes and how to avoid them. Moneyweb.
https://www.moneyweb.co.za/moneyweb-
opinion/soapbox/common-money-saving-
mistakes-and-how-to-avoid-them/

McKenna, K. (2020, March 23). *Here's How*
You'll Know It's A Good Time To Invest. Forbes.
https://www.forbes.com/sites/kristinmckenna
/2020/03/23/heres-how-youll-know-its-a-
good-time-to-invest/?sh=795d6acb47a4

Mian, N. (2020, March 16). *The Pros & Cons of*
Investing in Commodities. ShariaPortfolio.
https://shariaportfolio.com/the-pros-cons-of-
investing-in-commodities/

Michael, G. (2021, March 3). *The 3 Best*
Commodities in Which to Invest. Investopedia.
https://www.investopedia.com/financial-
edge/0412/the-3-best-commodities-to-invest-
in.aspx

Minster, C. (2012, December 6). *The Lost*
Treasure of the Inca. ThoughtCo.

https://www.thoughtco.com/lost-treasure-of-the-inca-2136548

Minster, C. (2015). *10 Facts About the Spanish Conquistadors.* ThoughtCo. https://www.thoughtco.com/facts-about-the-spanish-conquistadors-2136511

Moskowitz, D. (2019). *Deflate Inflation with These 9 Assets.* Investopedia. https://www.investopedia.com/articles/investing/081315/9-top-assets-protection-against-inflation.asp

Motley Fool Staff. (2015, September 4). *What Kind of Investment Accounts Earn Compound Interest?* The Motley Fool. https://www.fool.com/knowledge-center/what-kind-of-investment-accounts-earn-compound-int.aspx

National Association of Realtors. (2020). 2020 Home Buyers and Sellers Generational Trends Report. www.nar.realtor. https://www.nar.realtor/sites/default/files/documents/2020-generational-trends-report-03-05-2020.pdf

Nguyen, J. (2019). *4 Key Factors That Drive the Real Estate Market.* Investopedia. https://www.investopedia.com/articles/mortgages-real-estate/11/factors-affecting-real-estate-market.asp

OnProperty. (2013, March 12). *12 Pros and Cons of Investing In Property.* On Property.

https://onproperty.com.au/pros-and-cons-of-investing-in-property/

Outlets, M. N., credit, government agencies S. committed to helping readers like you make informed, & Kossman, personal finance decisions R. T. B. editorial policies S. (n.d.). *The History of Credit Cards: Ancient Times to Present Day.* The Balance. https://www.thebalance.com/history-of-credit-cards-4766953

Patterson, G., & Aesop. (1988). *The goose that laid the golden egg.* Pan Books.

PowerofPositivity. (2021, March 16). *15 Behaviors That Attract More Positivity Into Your Life.* Power of Positivity: Positive Thinking & Attitude. https://www.powerofpositivity.com/more-positivity-behaviors-law-attraction/

President Franklin Delano Roosevelt and the New Deal | Great Depression and World War II, 1929-1945 | U.S. History Primary Source Timeline | Classroom Materials at the Library of Congress | Library of Congress. (n.d.). Library of Congress, Washington, D.C. 20540 USA. https://www.loc.gov/classroom-materials/united-states-history-primary-source-timeline/great-depression-and-world-war-ii-1929-1945/franklin-delano-roosevelt-and-the-new-deal/

Pritchard, J. (2016). *Compound Interest Makes Your Investments Grow.* The Balance. https://www.thebalance.com/compound-interest-4061154

Professional Academy. (2015). *Marketing Theories Explained - Maslow's Hierarchy of Needs.* Professionalacademy.com; Professional Academy - Training & Qualifications for Professionals. https://www.professionalacademy.com/blogs-and-advice/marketing-theories-maslows-hierarchy-of-needs

Read, J. (2016, July 15). *How the Great Fire of London created insurance.* Museum of London. https://www.museumoflondon.org.uk/discove r/how-great-fire-london-created-insurance#:~:text=This%20fire%20mark%20w as%20issued

Rosenberg, M. (2019). *The Major Sectors of the Economy.* ThoughtCo. https://www.thoughtco.com/sectors-of-the-economy-1435795

Scott, E. (2007, February 19). *Understanding and Using The Law of Attraction In Your Life.* Verywell Mind; Verywellmind. https://www.verywellmind.com/understanding -and-using-the-law-of-attraction-3144808

Seeger, M. L. (1978). Media of Exchange in 16th Century New Spain and the Spanish

Response. *The Americas*, *35*(2), 168–184. https://doi.org/10.2307/980902

Seppala, E. (2019, October 21). *Debits & Credits | What They Are & Why They Matter*. Merchant Maverick. https://www.merchantmaverick.com/debits-and-credits-explained/#:~:text=A%20debit%20is%20an%20accounting

Siebold, S. (2016, April 19). *I'm a self-millionaire— here are 7 things I think everyone should understand about money*. Business Insider. https://www.businessinsider.com/7-things-i-think-everyone-should-understand-about-money-2016-4?IR=T#-8

Storrs, C. (2011). *"The "Decline" of Spain in the Seventeenth Century*. https://doi.org/

Taylor, B. (2019). *The Costs of Investing*. Investopedia. https://www.investopedia.com/investing/costs-investing/

TED. (2020, February 10). *6 ways to improve your relationship with money | The Way We Work, a TED series*. YouTube. https://www.youtube.com/watch?v=s0H1jxF5TWQ

The Best Countries to Invest In. (2021). @USNews. https://www.usnews.com/news/best-countries/best-countries-to-invest-in

The College Investor. (2018, April 23). *Investing Fees Explained! How Honest Financial Advisors Should Disclosure Their Fees.* YouTube. https://www.youtube.com/watch?v=5KLEgkfR_2Y

The Infographics Show. (2018, May 28). *Insurance Explained - How Do Insurance Companies Make Money and How Do They Work.* YouTube. https://www.youtube.com/watch?v=qjXgpJpSlCc

United Nations. (2020). *World Investment Report 2020.*

Wayne, C. (2020, November 19). *Financial Literacy - A Beginners Guide to Financial Education.* YouTube. https://www.youtube.com/watch?v=4XZIv4_sQA

Wealth Definition. (2019). Investopedia. https://www.investopedia.com/terms/w/wealth.asp

Why does money have so much power? (2017, October 23). HR Future. https://www.hrfuture.net/talent-management/personal-development/why-does-money-have-so-much-power/

You Will Love Economics. (2018). Macro Minute -- Bond Prices and Interest Rates YouTube. https://www.youtube.com/watch?v=WAqLZe-iEWA

Your Youniverse. (2017, November 26). *How to ALIGN With The ENERGY Of MONEY & ABUNDANCE - POWERFUL Law of Attraction Technique!* YouTube. https://www.youtube.com/watch?v=xXPYjE8 o-rI

Zoe Financial. (2020, August 18). *The Importance of Time in the Market vs Timing the Market.* Www.prnewswire.com. https://www.prnewswire.com/news-releases/the-importance-of-time-in-the-market-vs-timing-the-market-301113822.html

Printed in Great Britain
by Amazon